The Angel Babies Leviathan IIII
Angelus Domini

~*~

I N S P I R I T* A S P I R E* E S P R I T* I N S P I R E*

Because of the things that have first become proclaimed within the spirit, and then translated into the soul, in order for the body to then become alive and responsive or to aspire, or to be inspired, if only then for the body to become a vessel, or a catalyst, or indeed an instrument of will, with which first the living spirit that gave life to it, along with the merits and the meaning of life, and the instruction and the interpretation of life, is simply to understand that the relationship between the spirit and the soul, are also the one living embodiment with which all things are one, and become connected and interwoven by creating, or causing what we can come to call, or refer to as the essence, or the cradle, or the fabric of life, which is in itself part physical and part spirit.

And so it is, that we are all brought into being, along with this primordial and spiritual birth, and along with this the presence or the origins of the spirit, which is also the fabric and the nurturer of the soul with which the body can be formed, albeit that by human standards, this act of nature however natural, can now take place through the act of procreation or consummation, and so it is with regard to this living spirit that we are also upon our natural and physical birth, given a name and a number, inasmuch that we represent, or become identified by a color, or upon our created formation and distinction of identity, we become recognized by our individuality.

But concerning the Angels, it has always been of an interest to me how their very conception, or existence, or origin from nature and imagination, that they could have become formed and brought into being, as overtime I have heard several stories of how with the event of the first creation of man, that upon this event, that all the Angels were made to accept and to serve in God's creation of man, and that man was permitted to give command to these Angels in the event of his life, and the trials of his life which were to be mastered, but within this godly decree and narrative, we also see that there was all but one Angel that either disagreed or disapproved with, not only the creation of man, but also with the formation of this covenant between God and man, and that all but one Angel was Satan, who was somewhat displeased with God's creation of man, and in by doing so would not succumb or show respect or demonstrate servility or humility toward man or mankind.

As overtime it was also revealed to me that with the creation of the Angels, that it was also much to their advantage as it was to ours, for the Angels themselves to adhere to this role and to serve in the best interest of man's endeavors upon the face of the earth, as long as man himself could demonstrate and become of a will and a nature to practice his faith with a spirit, and a soul, and a body that would become attuned to a godly or godlike nature, and in by doing so, and in by believing so, that all of his needs would be met with accordingly.

And so this perspective brings me to question my own faith and ideas about the concept and the ideology of Angels, insomuch so that I needed to address and to explore my own minds revelation, and to investigate that which I was told or at least that which I thought I knew concerning the Angels along with the juxtaposition that if Satan along with those Angels opposed to serving God's creation of man, and of those that did indeed seek to serve and to favor God's creation and to meet with the merits, and the dreams, and the aspirations of man, that could indeed cause us all to be at the mercy and the subjection of an externally influential and internal spiritual struggle or spiritual warfare, not only with ourselves, but also with our primordial and spiritual identity.

And also because of our own conceptual reasoning and comprehension beyond this event, is that what we almost find ourselves astonished into believing is that this idea of rights over our mortal souls or being, must have begun or started long ago, or at least long before any of us were even souls inhabiting our physical bodies here as a living presence upon the face of the earth, and such is this constructed dilemma behind our beliefs or identities, or the fact that the names, or the numbers that we have all been given, or that have at least become assigned to us, is simply because of the fact that we have all been born into the physical world.

As even I in my attempts, have tried to attempt to come to terms with the very idea of how nature and creation could allow so many of us to question this reason of totality, if only for me in the present context deliver to you the story of the Angel Babies, if only to understand, or to restore, if your faith along with mine, back into the realms of mankind and humanity, as I have also come to reflect in my own approach and understanding of this narrative between God and Satan and the Angels, that also in recognizing that they all have the power to influence and to subject us to, as well as to direct mankind and humanity, either to our best or worst possibilities, if only then to challenge our primordial spiritual origin within the confines of our own lifestyles, and practices and beliefs, as if in our own efforts and practices that we are all each and every one of us, in subjection or at least examples and products of both good and bad influences.

Which is also why that in our spiritual nature, that we often call out to these heavenly and external Angelic forces to approach us, and to heal us, and to bless us spiritually, which is, or has been made to become a necessity, especially when there is a humane need for us to call out for their assistance, and their welfare, for the benefit of our own souls, and our own bodies to be aided or administered too, or indeed for the proper gifts to be bestowed upon us, to empower us in such a way, that we can receive guidance and make affirmations through the proper will and conduct of a satisfactory lesson learnt albeit through this practical application and understanding, if only to attain spiritual and fruitful lives.

As it is simply by recognizing that we are, or at some point or another in our lives, have always somewhat been open, or subject to the interpretations of spiritual warfare by reason of definition, in that Satan's interpretation of creation is something somewhat of contempt, in that God should do away with, or even destroy creation, but as much as Satan can only prove to tempt, or to provoke God into this reckoning, it is only simply by inadvertently influencing the concepts, or the ideologies of man, that of which whom God has also created to be creators, that man through his trials of life could also be deemed to be seen in Satan's view, that somehow God had failed in this act of creation, and that Satan who is also just an Angel, could somehow convince God of ending creation, as Satan himself cannot, nor does not possess the power to stop or to end creation, which of course is only in the hands of the creator.

And so this brings me back to the Angels and of those that are in favor of either serving, or saving mankind from his own end and destruction, albeit that we are caught up in a primordial spiritual fight that we are all engaged in, or by reason of definition born into, and so it is only by our choices that we ultimately pay for our sacrifice, or believe in our rights to life, inasmuch that we are all lifted up to our greatest effort of our design, if we can learn to demonstrate and to accept our humanity in a way that regards and reflects our greater desire or need to be something more than what we choose to believe in, which is only in the hands of God the creator or indeed a spirit in the sky.

SYNOPSIS

It was very much my intention not to state the name of any particular place in the script as I thought that the telling of the story of the Angel Babies is in itself about believing in who you are, and also about facing up to your fears. The Angel Babies is also set loosely in accordance with the foretelling of the Bibles Revelations.

I thought it would be best to take this approach, as the writing of the script is also about the Who, What, Where, When, How and Why scenario that we all often deal with in our ongoing existence. It would also not be fair to myself or to anyone else who has read the Angel Babies to not acknowledge this line of questioning, for instance, who are we? What are we doing here? Where did we come from? And when will our true purpose be known? And how do we fulfil our true potential to better ourselves and others, the point of which are the statements that I am also making in the Angel Babies and about Angels in particular,

Is that if we reach far into our minds we still wonder Where did the Angels come from and what is their place in this world. I know sometimes that we all wish and pray for the miracle of life to reveal itself but the answer to this mystery truly lives within us and around us, I only hope that you will find the Angel Babies an interesting narrative and exciting story as I have had in bringing it to life, after all there could be an Angel Baby being born right now.

INSPIRIT* ASPIRE* ESPRIT* INSPIRE*

The Angel Babies Story, was very much written and inspired by many feelings of expression, that were buried very deeply inside of me, as it was through my own exchanges and relationships and journeying, and upon discovery of both negative and positive aspects of experiences, that often challenged my own beliefs, and personal expectations of what I thought or felt was my own life's purpose and reason for being and doing, and very much what any one of us would expect, to be the result or the outcome of their own personal life choices based upon the status quo of our own design or choosing.

The story within itself, very much maintains its own conception of intercession from one person to another, as we can only contain the comprehension of the things that are most viable and of course what we most relate too, and that which most commonly resemble and reflects our emotions and experiences, in being something tangible that either connects or resonate at will deeply within us, as many of us have the ability and intuit nature, to grasp things not merely as they are presented to us, but how things can also unfold and manifest in us that are sometimes far beyond our everyday imaginings, and that are also equally hard to grasp and somewhat difficult to comprehend and let alone explain.

As we often learn to see such challenges and difficulties as these, especially in young minds that react and are often gifted, or equally find it in themselves in life changing circumstances, to naturally have or bear a gift when it comes to dealing with prevailing situations, that most of us would often take for granted, or would naturally see as the average norm, as we are all somewhat uniquely adjusted to deal with the same prevailing situation very differently, or even more so to uniquely perceive it in very different ways.

As for the question of how we all independently learnt to communicate through these various means of creative, or artistic, or spiritual measures, is also simply a way of communicating to God as in prayer, as well as with one another, as all aspects are one of the same creation, as to whether such forms of expression can personify, or act as an intermediate medium or channel to God, or indeed from one person to another, is again very much dependent upon the nature of its composition and expression, and the root from which it extends, and so for us to believe that our forebearers, or indeed our ancestors have the ability to intercede for us in such spiritual terms upon this our journey through life, is very much to say, that it is through their life's experiences, that we have become equipped, and given a wealth, and a portion of their life's history, with which for us to make our own individual efforts and choices, for us to be sure and certain of the way, in which we shall eventually come to be.

Time is neither here or there, it is a time in between time as it is the beginning and yet the end of time. This is a story of the Alpha and the Omega, the first and the last and yet as we enter into this revelation, we begin to witness the birth of the Angel Babies a time of heavenly conception when dying Angels gave birth to Angelic children who were born to represent the order of the new world. The names of these Angel Babies remained unknown but they carried the Seal of their fathers written on their foreheads, and in all it totalled one hundred and forty four thousand Angels and this is the story of one of them.

They say that the Angels dwell and reside just beyond the mid points of the firmament, and the unseen world between the Heavens and the Earth, they say there are Legends written and spoken off across the ages and many are called but few are chosen, and whilst my life is full and complete and yet there is little I have achieved or even cared to have challenged, and I do not claim to possess the key that could set mankind free or even set my life on a true course to fulfill my own or anyone else's destiny.

So seldom are the descendants of the ascended Angels mentioned, but here on Earth in my home and domain I can see many symbolic representations and manifestations of the very legacy to which I belong too, and bearing upon this land which has been fought over for many a legacy and legend, shall always remain present but forever untold, for our true story is only written in and upon the hearts of those who know us, but do not necessarily know our presence or our names

Ext: As Stefan set out to fly south, all the memories of his entire life flashed like images in front of his eyes, flooding into his veins swelling with energy, resounding and pushing upon his will, as he was now re-awakening and empowering his mind, his feelings and his emotions, surging with new life waking his soul and strengthening his love for none other than that of his beloved

Ext: Somewhere between oblivion and the sea of souls, Stefan is now flying with the wings of fire, with a passionate will of determined desire to push back the murky, muddy, darkened depths like a tsunami preparing to unleash its' wrath upon the unsuspecting creatures beneath, whipping up a torrent now rising up into the treacherous blackened skies above, like a fountain of fury disturbing the sea of souls in their sudden cry and the awakening of none other than the angel of the abyss, and the depths below, now rising out of the sea of souls, shimmering like a watery diamond with the souls of the lost and the damned, all sea like and translucently formless in its' appearance of something glistening, like liquid mercury born out of an anger that rages both empty and endless, consuming all in its path as though nothing ever could.

Angel Of The Abyss

You cannot change the laws of creation, son of Hark, nor can you undo thc depths of the abyss, your presence here shakes the very sands of the bottomless sea's these wings of fire that you possess are a curse and a judgment to me, your every trial will cause the earth to shake from within and upon itself, have you no concern of what will happen once you arrive to the other world, all shall be endangered by the very justice you so carelessly flap and fly with, so long as you have these wings I cannot permit you to pass, think of your loved ones and spare them this quest for mortal love, instead join me and come to know the belly of the soulless sea's deep beneath, let me douse the flames and put an end to this endless passion for desire

Stefan Stiles

I have been released and freed from my own doing, I have been granted another chance and it is by this clemency of exoneration that is mines to bare and mine alone, for if I am released from the boundless depths of oblivion, then I have also freed those with whom have felt that I held them captive for so very long and no doubt if a judgment is to be passed then let me fly homeward as each of us must eventually come to rest in a place that echoes and reflects a peace from within, I cannot hold the world in contempt for something it knows not of itself, nor can these flames be put out by a tempestuous sea that is drowning in its own sorrow

Angel Of The Abyss

Then I bid you farewell and good luck but don't say that I didn't warn you, for your wrath upon us may be a judgment unsurpassable, if you do not comprehend what it is you know not of yourself

Stefan Stiles

I know this much and I am not yet satisfied
with the toils of my struggle and plight

Angel Of The Abyss

Then listen well for in the mountains that stand before you, I must
warn you that as vast as they are and as wide as I am and yet still
they do not bow to the treacherous sea of souls below, but little by
little and spec by spec even they shall eventually crumble and fall
piece by piece like the dust in these sands that are now scattered
beneath me, even unto me the seas I am patient and I am just for I
know in time they will crumble and fall to me

Stefan Stiles

You may be assured of one thing my friend but I cannot wait around
to see what stories time has to tell, as we may all very well yield to
you in time and you may be superior in these midst, but as for now
the mountains still stand albeit of stubborn rock and stone

Angel Of The Abyss

Stubborn!" stubborn rock and stone, you amuse me, maybe you should
go and see the one who pulls down the rigid rock from its' high and
mighty places, for it is only I who has truly seen the mountain move

Ext: As Stefan moved at speed and will over the mountainous regions, even the ground and rocky terrains below seem to shake and tremble with the sound of gravity's anger forever pulling and weighing at him to yield to the plains beneath him, even the soiled earth did give way and fall into the cracks and craters of the now bellowing opening ground, swallowing up bodies of the Earth, until ridge ways burst open sending up sulphurous smoke into the air laden with moltenous debris arising from its' summit, creating luminous arcs and plumes of volcanic ash. Ext: When Stefan neared the mountain top, even their roofs did give way, spitting out molten lave into the skies above while sending down rivers hot molten lava along the mountain face into various cracks and crevices, creating fiery rivulets down the regions of its' slopes, down into the soulless sea below, as this was to be the beginning of Stefan's trial as he heard a voice coming from deep within the well of the mountain.

Angel Of The Abyss

Even now as you arrive, your presence is known amongst the saint's and the prophets and the entire household of heaven to bear witness to your trial

Stefan Stiles

Who are you, what bewilderment is this?

Angel Of The Abyss

Who is a liar, but he who denies the truth

Stefan Stiles

I deny nothing, this is the past you speak of, reveal yourself to me,
I command you too

Angel Of The Abyss

For many deceivers have gone out into the world who do not confess

Stefan Stiles

But why, why am I being judged, I have served have I not, I have
sipped from the cup of iniquity and poured out its judgment,
what wrath can be put upon me now

Angel Of The Abyss

They shall no more offer their sacrifices after whom this shall be a
statue forever for them to judge throughout their generation

**Ext: Just then the mountain erupted with a violent and raging
explosion, and Stefan was caught up unawares and swallowed
by the sheer power of the force, then he suddenly fell spiraling
downward into the belly of the mountain, fearing for his life and
his vulnerability to the terrifying and eruptive elements below,
even as the moltenous seas flooded onto the mountains core,
covering Stefan from head to toe, into a caste of burning lava
ridden with the sands and the debris of the soulless sea, which
quickly began to solidify, as the seas hardened into a caste of
rock around him, creating a shell of an imprisonment, and then
again with the waters slowly rising and flooding over this caged
angelic statue, with only the angel of the abyss as its' keeper.**

Angel Of The Abyss

They sacrificed to demons not to God, but to god's they did not know, to new god's, new arrivals that your father did not fear, if Satan cast out Satan then he is divided against himself, how then will his kingdom stand

Ext: As the angel of the abyss spoke out of the murky depths to the entrapped angelic figure, now slowly drowning inside the well of the mountain, the souls of the sea began to emerge taking on the form of sand creatures hardened and deadened by the molten lava, now creating a mist of sulphurous gases, although small in stature there were many of them, too many to be controlled or defeated by an angel now imprisoned in a caste of rock and debris, they began by pulling Stefan down into the depths below as commanded by the angel of the abyss.

Angel Of The Abyss

Pull! Pull! Pull him down

Ext: Stefan now fell like a rock of Goliath into the sands of the seabed floor, now caught up and bounded by the reeds and weeds, being pulled even further and deeper beneath the seabed floor, until there was no longer any sign of him to be seen.

Angel Of The Abyss

Unless Satan takes advantage of us we are not ignorant of his devices.

Ext: As the angel of the abyss uttered these final words, Stefan's cage and caste was completely swallowed up, disappearing below and beneath the dark engulfing murky watery sands, all was now but still, as if nothing had happened but for one momentary second three particles of light began rising up and filtering through the sand and the waters, rising higher and higher into the oblivious skies above, containing only the elemental remnants of Stefan's heart, mind and soul.

Ext: Now imagine being suspended high in flight over the earth and below the heavens above, looking both up toward the stratosphere and down toward the earthly plains and horizons below, whilst having the scope and the capacity to gaze all around you, while taking in the view with each and every breath, in every moment and thought, realizing that time itself was unfolding before you, revealing in your awakening senses, each and every soul that you may ever have transcended or encountered within your lifetime, almost searching and seeking where to fly to next upon this heavenly journey, in and amongst the clouds in the skyline, drifting and sailing along, as if being ferried like timeless memories on a voyage within an infinite spirit, sailing towards the light, thinking of where to descend to next, or simply in anticipation upon the event of readiness to begin your descent, to find what might be your next sanctuary or resting place once this flight had cease upon its searching, and once this place called Nejeru, had called out to you from afar, somehow knowingly you had felt that you had arrived and entered into the enlightening realms of the Tetra valley, whilst simply forgetting that the remnants and traces of where you have been and what you have become have left their stain and mark upon the bottomless pit of the Abyss, causing other mysterious creatures to be formed and appear from the forgotten depths of this desolate and wretched place, that is unforgiving of its' own soul to feed upon.

Ext; For what Stefan Stiles did not now know was that for every action there would be a reaction, as when he had struggled for his freedom and liberation from the angel of the abyss, as it was that during his death and resurrection, was that it was his life force and that of which is of an Angelic substance, had allowed the creatures of the deep to draw upon and take sustenance from his natural form of purity, almost igniting and erupting them into life, causing mere simple creatures to feed upon his life force whilst giving them strength and power and vigor and a life support system of their own, whilst causing them to grow and become monstrous in their appearance, but also equally allowing them to receive great strength and ability, to leap and to fly high above the mountainous regions of the deep and gain mastery over the skies and the regions of the Seas, as such was a monstrous creature that had come and leapt forth from the deep, that had justly nurtured itself upon the energies that Stefan Stiles had indeed left behind in his tracks and the pursuit to wake and ascend towards his transformation, but even unbeknowingly so, this creature was already hungry and ably apt and ready to feed upon any substance which was of an Angelic kind to say the least in order to nurture and feed itself, as this creature formed, was soon now to be known as Leviathan.

Ext: As it was that some time after three particles of lights containing the elemental remnants of Stefan's heart, mind and soul had ascended into the realms of the heavenly abode, that a fishing vessel that was by now set assail nearby, trawling the seas for marine life had unknowingly disturbed the lair of the creature beneath, and so it was that as these fishermen and their ship sailed over the waters, that something began to stir beneath the deep below, making the waves become more and more aggressively violent and disruptive by the movement and motion of the awaking Leviathan now steadily swimming up to the water's surface, agitated by the influence of the ships engine above.

Ext: And so it was that before the unsuspecting fishermen in their vessel could prepare themselves from the upheaval and onslaught of an instant and direct collision of their ship up against the sudden and ferocious might and impact of the now emerging and forceful Leviathan, so much so that they were tossed up into the air as the ship rocked off balance to and fro, throwing them all overboard and into the surrounding sea, as it was then that the Leviathan had capsized the ship along with the fishermen whilst becoming airborne above them and released from its' lair beneath the deep abyss, the Leviathan now swinging its' tail around to now see its' victims panicking and struggling in the waters attempting to stay afloat, let out a mighty roar of sulphur upon them from its' mouth, covering the fishermen in soars and blisters with burns and boils forming upon their faces and hands before it eventually took off high into flight above the sea in its' advance to find the scent and the trail of its' own Angelic spawning and yet by now somewhat possessed and hungry soul.

Ext: The Leviathan was by now hot on the trails and tracking the time signature elementally locked within the ether that Stefan Stiles had unknowingly left behind in his wake, eclipsing the Sun against its' shadowy wingspan and in cold blooded pursuit of a savagery hunger to find and feed upon its' unsuspecting angelic prey, as for now the Leviathan had already transcended and had breached what was once far beyond its' unending horizon that had once separated one realm called Oblivion and the mountains of the abyss from the other place, as it had by now flown within the realms and the reality of the earth's sphere of influence that would indeed lead it to uncover the Holy and final physical resting place of none other than that of Stefan's Mother, Selah, where once stood Josephine and Angelo Stiles, along with Mercidiah, where they had once witnessed Stefan's transformation and rebirth, in what was by now an unkempt and neglected and untidy dilapidated place called Godstone Cemetery.

Ext: And so it was to be the cause of a rippling effect throughout the realms of the lower heavens and that of the earthly sphere as Leviathan drew near to Godstone Cemetery, that its' very essence of presence would resound and awaken and intuitively set off spiritual alarm bells, that would easily be sensed by any Earth Mother, that would happen to keeping watch and vigil over this domain, as well as be very much prepared over such unlikely occurrences to happen, and yet as it did occur, so too did Kali Ma become alert and attuned in her senses to become switched on to such mysterious and compelling forces of activity, and by doing so, her first point of reaction and response was to call upon the covenant of that of the Sisterly hierarchy of the Earth Mothers to inform them that something looming was by now becoming very much imminent.

Int: And as if it were somehow to be some long awaited prediction of a fulfillment of a prophecy that were somehow announced long, long ago, and seemingly so, as within the expectation of these Mothers of Earth held in their belief and faith of expecting the unexpected, for as soon as this female matriarchal had collectively come together as a secret association in order to fulfill a pact, it could only be then, that what they would be set to do what they were taught to do, for them to comprehend the true gravity and severity of the present danger now being presented to them, to find the answer if not the solutions in equating this arising problem.

Int: Once Again the Earth Mothers find themselves collectively congregating in the house known as Madam Madinique, Specialist in Tarot Readings, Palmistry, Fortune Telling, Clairvoyant and Spiritualist, at the request and invitation of Kali Ma, and now also amongst them as a fully fledged Sister of the Earth Mothers, Josephine Stiles.

Kali Ma

I fear that something evil has arisen from out of the abyss my Sisters and I sense that it is of a direct threat to that of the Earth Angels

Mercidiah

But what could pose such a threat Kali, is it as we have feared, something born out of the one that could threaten the heavens

Kali Ma

I am not so sure Merci, except that it possesses the same influential power that we have come across before, which is also similar to that of the Earth Angels, but yes I also sensed that it is also possessed of the one that could threaten the heavens, but might I also say my Sisters that anything which arises out of the Abyss of oblivion, is a threat to the heavens, and of course is not a good sign or omen to any of us concerned

Mercidiah

Come let us form a circle and join hands, and see what we can fathom from the Earthly sphere that influences us

Int: And so it was that the Earth Mothers made a circle and reached out to one another in joining hands and set about closing their eyes to begin their perfected meditation, and soon afterwards as equal members, they had entered into a deep hypnotic trance, that would eventually transcend them into the earthly sphere and state of influence where the heavens reveal its' secrets of dictates to the earth, and where the earth is also equally responsive to the heavens, and so as they bonded together within this one unique marriage complimenting each other within the universe that holds them within the sustainment of all living creatures and beings of life, they began to witness above and beyond the natural order of things.

Int: As for now the vision was becoming revealed to them, although somewhat cloaked and disguised in an unfathomable incoherent way, where angels seemed to be engaged in a battle fighting alongside each other to subdue and to overcome the Leviathan, but somewhere in the midst of all this mayhem and confusion was Stefan Stiles, trapped and somewhat threatened by this devouring beast, with no sign of defending himself or defeating this foe, and so it was that as he toiled and struggled endlessly to defend against the onslaught and attack, it would seem that his fate would soon come to an horrific and tragic end, in becoming ferociously torn limb from limb and then devoured by the Leviathan, except that before the horror could be truly witnessed and attested too, Josephine let out a mighty and deadly scream as she broke away from the circle of the Earth Mothers as she couldn't bear to watch this nightmare any longer, as she began to cry and weep helplessly, as if indeed her beloved Stefan's fate were already somehow written within the context of this revealing vision.

Kali Ma

Save your tears Josephine, for this was only a vision of the things that might or mighten happen

Josephine Stiles

But I saw what happened, we all did

Mercidiah

No Josey, we did not see what happened inasmuch that it is a warning of what will happen or might take place if we do nothing to prevent it from happening

Kali Ma

It would seem that this no ordinary or mortal sea monster, If it can be of a challenging trial in its wake in wreaking havoc and causing desecration upon the Earth Angels

Josephine Stiles

But what must we do Kali Ma to defeat and prevent this brutal annihilation of the Earth Angels, if they are so threatened by this creature?

Mercidiah

She is right Kali Ma, we cannot allow for the Earth Angels to be put in harm's way like this, to be desecrated and brought down and slaughtered like prey by this Leviathan

Kali Ma

Well to be sure, I believe that this creature can only truly be defeated by the immortality of an Angel of pure essence and one of true distinction from the rest

Mercidiah

Well what does that mean Kali, by that description it seems that you must mean a Herald Angel?

Kali Ma

Yes! I do, I'm afraid to say it so, but in this matter I believe only A Herald Angel may be able to defeat such a creature

Josephine Stiles

Well what about Hark, surely he can defeat such a beast as this

Kali Ma

I am not so sure if he is the one, or even if it is possible for us to engage with Hark the Herald Angel in this matter Josephine

Josephine Stiles

Well why not, I mean after all, it is his Son and my soulmates life that is at stake at here

Mercidiah

Well why not Hark Kali, I mean who else could possesses such an essence of purity other than he?

Josephine Stiles

Answer her Kali who, who else can you call into this campaign to defeat such a beast

Kali Ma

Well with some reservations and doubts and regret, I believe that besides Hark, there is only one other Herald that I would consider in such a crisis and matter

Josephine Stiles

Who, tell us?

Kali Ma

Ophlyn!

Josephine Stiles

Ophlyn! Are you mad, that's absurd, and he is just as much as a monster as anything else

Kali Ma

My point exactly

Mercidiah

But what do you hope to achieve Kali, and where are you going with this, I mean he after all he is declared removed and resigned to the soul cages, and he is immensely untrustworthy and somewhat unpredictable

Kali Ma

Yes, but if we are to destroy a greater evil and threat to the
Earth Angels, then Ophlyn would be the right choice and
candidate to do it, as by now his soul will be pure, strong,
redefined and undefined and untampered with, and untainted
by any defects through the transmigrations that he has already
endured, as for Hark, it may be too much of a task and trial to
be called to tackle such a matter, and also come to think of it,
also Zyxven springs to mind

Mercidiah

Zyxven, but what about Zyxven, why would you think to suggest
that he could play a part in all of this, suppose he is put in danger
and harm's way, no I don't want him involved, think of something
else Kali

Kali Ma

Wait Merci, do not be so quick to fret and to fear, just listen and pay
attention for a moment, as I truly believe that Zyxven can be relied
upon in such a task

Mercidiah

But how, he is inexperienced, and he has never before fought to
claim any such distinctions in flight or battle

Kali Ma

Yes I know Merci, but he is a thinker, a philosopher, a diplomat and a debater, and he has the power of the truth and the word upon his side, and I think that we may also need him to take up such a challenge, as he may prove useful with his prophetic tongue in binding up and exorcising any malicious forms of Angelic substances that the Leviathan may possess

Josephine Stiles

Yes that is true, but how do we set about reawakening Ophlyn to see if he is even willing to do our bidding in this ridiculous preposterous ordeal, without us being entirely sure if he may want to take revenge and retribution upon us all, and what about Stefan?

Kali Ma

Well it seems that it is highly likely that above all of this, that it is Stefan's life that is at the very heart of the matter, and so we must therefore make preparations to defend and protect him at all costs

Josephine Stiles

But as we already know, that Stefan fought with Ophlyn's Son Ruen, so how can we honestly be sure and certain that once we free him, that he will not take revenge and feed Stefan's body to the Leviathan to avenge his son's death?

Mercidiah

Well that may be so, but the truth is that we do not know what Ophlyn's actions may determine in this campaign if we free him from the soul cages, but if we idly sit by and do nothing, then ultimately the outcome will be the same, and undoubtedly we already know what will happen if we choose not to act in this matter Josey

Josephine Stiles

But do you honestly know what you're doing Kali Ma, because I don't think you do

Kali Ma

Well what will you have me do differently Sister, and what would you do to increase Stefan's chances of survival under these circumstances?

Josephine Stiles

Well I wouldn't conjure up Ophlyn's soul from beyond the crypt, and I wouldn't put my own beloved husband's or Mercidiah's only child's life at risk or in jeopardy over this

Kali Ma

So what would you suggest Josephine, do you honestly think that it will work out by itself if we sit by and watch things as they unfold in front of our eyes, while this sea monster starts to wreak havoc and destruction in its' wake until it finally comes to feast upon the house of Hark, I mean afterall it is your beloveds line above all else that is at risk here and in harm's way, if Leviathan finds Stefan, then it will also find Hark and even Angelo, and even if we may directly be in some danger because of it, of course I know what is at stake and what I am doing

Mercidiah

Yes you do don't you Kali Ma, and I to now know what you intend to do, but are you sure that you want it to be this way, I mean what if we wake Ophlyn's soul to find that it is not as you had thought, what then?

Kali Ma

Then I will suffer the consequences and do whatever it is in my power and necessary for me to bring this matter to a conclusion, but if I am right, then I believe in my heart that we shall all benefit from this decision and that everything shall work out for the best for all of us

Mercidiah

Once again I put it to you plainly Kali, are you sure that you want to do this?

Kali Ma

Yes Merci I am sure, I am sure that it is his will

Mercidiah

Well then I'm afraid to say that in spite of everything, that you sincerely haven my blessing but upon the bond of our sisterly love and friendship I appreciate that you must make this summons independently, as neither you nor I can overly involve Josephine or indeed myself if it is your sole decision to pursue this course of action if in anyway…

Kali Ma

Yes Merci, I understand If indeed in any way it may turn out or become linked to either of you, that it may have any irreparable consequences for the both of you I do understand, but just so that you know, I have already made up my mind to do this alone and once again I thank you for your vote of confidence and for your blessing and understanding in this matter, now both of you go, go and leave me and find and be with Stefan, until I have fulfilled the rest of my bargaining

Ext: Now shortly after penetrating and piercing its' way through the never ending horizon, the trail and the scent of Angel Stefan which had by now led the Leviathan through to the Godstone Cemetery, where this beast of a sea monster was now frantically searching and foraging through these hallowed and forgotten grounds, recklessly and haphazardly and flippantly knocking and turning over grave stones, as it scratched away with its coarse and scaly hardened talons, digging away and unearthing its way through grave after grave, looking for detectful clues of what it would soon come to discover as being the place of Selah's burial chamber, which was by now partially obstructed and hidden by some overgrown weeds and bushes of wilted and wild flowers, where the scent of an inherent and hereditary bloodline that still remained and lingered ever present in the damp musky mildew air, could still be smelt and sniffed away at by this creature of the abyss.

Ext: But as for when the Leviathan attempted in its efforts to scratch away and uncover the tombstone and burial place of Selah's chamber, so too did a shadowy silhouetted figure appear without exceeding or having any real physical or substantial form within it, and so it was that as the Leviathan could advance and forage no further, in being and becoming somewhat sustained and held in its tracks, as if it had become obedient by a transient will of this now ever present ghostly figure, somehow defending the grave stone against the Leviathan now rearing itself rampantly back and forth and up and down, whilst attempting to fight and resist against this spell of restraint and control, and yet in being somewhat pacified in its' pursuits, the Leviathan continued to struggle and fought to be loosened and unbounded and unchastened by this immediate and invisible force, now somewhat momentarily appearing to tame it and keep it at bay.

Int: And so once again with Kali Ma the Dream of the Angel Babies began, as time is neither here or there, as it is a time in between time as it is the beginning and yet the end of time as this is a story of the Alpha and the Omega, the first and the last and yet as we enter into this revelation, we begin to witness the birth of the Angel Babies a time of heavenly conception when dying angels gave birth to angelic children who were born to represent the order of the new world, the names of these Angel Babies remained unknown but they carried the Seal of their fathers written on their foreheads, and in all it totalled one hundred and forty four thousand Angels and this is the story of one of them, as they say that the Angels dwell and reside just beyond the mid points of the firmament, and the unseen world between the Heavens and the Earth, they say there are Legends written and spoken off across the ages of time, and many are called but few are chosen, and whilst my life is full and complete and yet there is little I have achieved or even cared to have challenged, and I do not claim to possess the key that could set mankind free or even set my life on a true course to fulfill my own or anyone else's purpose and destiny.

Kali Ma

Yin Men Shen, I chant thee the incantation of Yin Men Shen, guardians
of the door, obey me and free thy servant Angelus Domini Ophlyn
from this the Animatism of thy Cavea, and break the doctrine of the
Otachuk Cavea Jiva, O Veni Liberate Angelus Ophlyn Jiva Cavea!

Guardians Of The Door

Who is the whisperer of these ancient names,
and what is your purpose, and why are you here?

Kali Ma

It is I Kali Ma

Guardians Of The Door

Otahchuk Cavea! You seeketh Angelus Ophlyn Domini from this Cavea of Yin Men Shen Jiva Otahchuk, reveal thyself and thy true purpose Kali

Kali Ma

O Veni Men Shen, Angelus Ophlyn Domini, Oportet Vivere Amo

Guardians Of The Door

Oportet Vivere, Men Shen Yin, Angelus Ophlyn Domini Otahchuk Cavea, Amo Amas, Amamus Amanot Ma kali?

Kali Ma

Yes I Yin Men Shen, I command thee to grant Angelus Ophlyn free and safe passage through this place to me!

Guardians Of The Door

O Veni Ma Kali, Descendi Amo Angelus Domini Ophlyn?

Kali Ma

Yes I Obey, Guardians of the Door, Amo I Ophlyn Angelus

Guardians Of The Door

Amo Amamus, Amanot Amant Angelus Ophlyn Ma Kali?

Kali Ma

Yes Guardian I love Angel Ophlyn

Int: Then from out of the concealment of a heavenly glow which came into Kali Ma's view, was the appearance of a celestial body emerging from within its own emittance of light and energy, as a faint and distant voice which by now began to speak from within this sphere of energy.

Angel Ophlyn

Kali Ma?

Kali Ma

Yes?

Angel Ophlyn

Vobis Oportet Vivere Ut Amo, you behove me to live for your love?

Kali Ma

Vero Herald Ut Amo, Yes Herald to love, Quo Amor Versus Tenuit Tenebit, those whom true love has held, it will go on holding

Angel Ophlyn

Ut Amo, to love, Non Sum Qualis Eram, I am not such as I was

Kali Ma

Ergo Quid Agis, Then how are you?

Angel Ophlyn

Cigito Ergo Sum, I think therefore I am

Kali Ma

Melius Ergo Mecum Veni, Very well then come with me

Int: Just then all fell silent as the room began to illuminate with bright flickering colours, twinkling like electric embers of light, dancing and forming all around one another as lively particles, and slowly but surely complementing each other as they burst into brilliant white lights of brightness, and then beginning to become aligned to each other, now starting to outline the form of a figure that were somehow reconfiguring to fulfill its' celestial body of what was by now appearing to be materializing as nothing other than that of the eventual soul, now emerging through these prisms of light coming together and being born before these instantaneous infinite particles, now found to be connecting to one another and interlocking into their constituents parts to make and transform themselves into the spiritual embodiment and then transforming themselves into the physical body and appearance of that which once was, and that which was now once again becoming into being, and known only as Ophlyn the Herald Angel.

Angel Ophlyn

Its' strange and yet it is funny, but I feel so alive, and reenergized by such a purifying immensity of life, coursing through my every being, and yet…

Kali Ma

And yet what Ophlyn?

Angel Ophlyn

And yet there is an element of an unknown depth and source of unequaled and yet unfathomable beginning and unimaginable impact of sorrows, that as of now are calling out to me from behind a veil of questionable and inquiring souls

Kali Ma

Yes that is because you have renewed not only yourself but also all that which you possess which is the ethereal breath of life, and yet as you say, it is also the questioning and the examination of the inquiring innumerable sorrow of souls, of that which also comes from within containing and sustaining the kiss death Herald

Int: As the seconds and the minutes and the hours of the day were seemingly no more different than the days with preceded before this day, but as for now, it was to be realized that for all of the days that had come to pass, so it was to be that for the first time, that Stefan the angelic Son of Hark the Herald Angel, and the now resurrected Ophlyn who was once also pronounced as an Herald Angel alongside Hark, who had by now become as a fallen Herald Angel, although once upon a time he also stood alongside Hark during the first harvest, was by now once more soon to come face to face with the Son of his one time sincerest friend and keeper and defender of the realm of the earth and that of the Angels of the Abode of the Empyreans, and soon to be inadvertently reminded in recognizing that at some point in time that in a past and previous life, that a chapter had been written, which had very much had played itself out much to the outcome of becoming the result of such a calamitous event that took place within the realms of this Angeldom, of being the consequence of something that which would historically be looked upon and reflected upon, and regarded as in the act of such a regrettable loss to all concerned, of both great and judgmental actions that would prove to hold all in contempt, and be witnessed for all to give a personal account to their own reflective counsel of their own consequential and determining individual choices of forceable engagement, which presented itself to be the outcome of their personal decisions in condemning Ophlyn to the Soul Cages.

Int: And so as Mercidiah and Josephine returned with Stefan back to the house and homestead of Madam Madinique to once again meet with and address their Mother Sister Kali Ma, who was by now formally reaffirming her ties with that of the restored and resurrected Ophlyn the Herald Angel, and so it was to be that upon their arrival that Stefan who was somewhat mystified and intensified with an overwhelming feeling of confusion and anguish and mixed emotions of guilt and trepidation as to what this encounter with Angel Ophlyn would entail to lead to in its outcome and prevalence, as so too did Mercidiah and Josephine somewhat fearfully and cautiously dread with anticipation in attempting to conceal their worries and concerns in knowing full well that they too would ultimately be powerless to interfere with, or to change any acts of aggression from Ophlyn towards Stefan if indeed any were to arise, or for them to even be able to begin to mediate with any degree of diplomacy to diffuse, or to prevent any hostilities, if indeed Ophlyn were to seek to attack or cause any affliction or harm toward Stefan in any shape or form.

Int: And so it was to be that upon their introduction and acquaintance, that as soon as the resurrected Ophlyn and Stefan Stiles the Son of Hark, had no sooner met with their eyes, that Ophlyn's feathered wings rippled and shuddered with an air of suspicion full of contempt and disdaining revilement, and then all of sudden Ophlyn leapt forward and grabbed Stefan by the throat in a locked stranglehold forcing him to the floor.

Angel Ophlyn

I know you, you are the merciless Son of Hark, and it was you that took my Son Ruen away from me, so tell how does it feel Son of Hark, and what kind of madness and folly of deception is this Kali Ma, why did you bring him here to insult to kill me is that your plan, and what do you all hope to gain in this fortune of play here, this half breed is no match for me

Stefan Stiles

No wait Ophlyn, please let me speak, let me explain

Angel Ophlyn

Explain what, the why the wherefore are no more to me now, this is your deception and trickery to attempt to do away with me, well now your judgment is mine, as you and your father have made sure of that, and so how can I Ophlyn pay heed to listen to your screams of pleading out to me as your enemy when you should die as you led my Son to die as an accursed and unwelcome sight before the household of this Angeldom, and now you appear before me, and come to me to torment me in my newly found moment of joy and freedom, while your presence here among mortal Women only stabs away at my heart and reminds me of the grief I have eternally suffered in the cages full of unrepentant and forgotten souls, when it was I Ophlyn, Herald to the Abode of the Angels, that was made to be bowed and broken and yielded to the disgust and the wastelands of the lowly and the wicked, and so now you too shall suffer and endure the same consequence of fate as I did Son of Hark, as it seems that while I slept that somehow in my absence that you have all developed a slothful smell of complacency and self born idle laziness about you, and yet it would seem that in your carelessness of self satisfaction and arrogance, that you have loosened a terrible affliction upon us, how very good of you to accommodate me and to offer me the upper hand in reigning and bringing down upon your heads my revenge and retribution

Stefan Stiles

Now is not the time to settle old scores Ophlyn,

Angel Ophlyn

Then when is the right time?

Stefan Stiles

If the heavens fall where shall we stand?

Angel Ophlyn

Well no doubt if the heavens fall, then the devil shall make work for your idle hands young foe

Stefan Stiles

You must learn from your erroneous ways Ophlyn and seek forgiveness and repatriation for your part in this Angeldom

Angel Ophlyn

And who are you to speak of repatriation and forgiveness when you took my Son away from me, is it not only right that you and Hark should pay the price and suffer a similar fate

Stefan Stiles

But your act was unjustified in this matter Ophlyn

Angel Ophlyn

Unjustified, unjustified, it seems that you hold yourself highly above this self righteous noble integrity that you speak of in high esteem young Angel, unjustified, but I am renewed and so therefore I am justified with fresh vigor and vitality running through my spirit, and I could so easily vanquish both you and your father Hark in the blink of an eye

Kali Ma

Stop this, stop this at once, I beg of you Stefan, I command you Ophlyn, Amo amas, Amat amamus Amatis, Amant! I Love, you love, he loves, we love, you love, they love, please see sense in this accursed nonsense and folly of your own choosing and making, if you desire to destroy each other for the benefit of nothing then so be it, and let it be, but Ophlyn listen to me now please, if you desire a Son of good intent and measure, and gracious and noble mind and spirit, then I shall give you what you want, if you so choose to accept me as your formal consummate Earth Mother, I urge you to reconsider and free him, save him for the greater good, hear my words Ophlyn, hear my plea for the sake of my bargaining and for the good of this Angeldom that you so proudly speak and represent of, I will be yours to yield a Son unto you, please Ophlyn, please let him go

Stefan Stiles

Me Paenitet Ophlyn, I am deeply sorry to see that you have suffered to see this unbearable loss of your beloved Son Ruen by my hand,

Angel Ophlyn

Thee Paenitet, you are sorry when the expression of your regret and remorse is received much too little and much too late for me

Stefan Stiles

Forgive me Ophlyn but I must say that there was a time when I thought or at least somehow felt that I too had truly died and that my time spell was finally over, but that was until I had become proven by the virtue of this resurrecting and one and only indefinable power of love, that had somehow influenced and transformed me, and brought me back from beneath the brink of darkness and returned my souls salvation back into the arms of my beloved

Angel Ophlyn

So you favour her over the call to arms?

Stefan Stiles

No Ophlyn I favour her, because she is the call to arms,
as are all Earth Mothers

Int: At that point during their exchange Angel Ophlyn loosened his grip around Stefan's throat and allowed him to stand upright.

Ext: And so as Angel Stefan and Ophlyn the Herald Angel attempted to reconcile their differences to each other as witnessed by Kali Ma, Josephine Stiles and Mercidiah, as the skies above the place known only as Madam Madinique also gave way to Angel Zyxven who came forth carrying with him, an open book that had been given over and handed to him, for the sake of the Empyreans, and so as he descended the veil that covered his face was once again removed to show and to give and to grant love and mercy for his namesake of that which is also the Sanctuary of Haven.

Angel Ophlyn

And who and what kind of creation of heaven are you?

Mercidiah

He is my Son

Angel Ophlyn

Your Son!

Angel Zyxven

Yes Merci is my Mother, and I am her consummate Son Zyxven, my Father is Simeon

Angel Ophlyn

Simeon you say, yes Simeon, and what kind of an Angel exactly of the Empyreans has Mercidiah and Simeon begotten?

Angel Zyxven

I am the sanctuary kind of begotten Haven of the Empyreans

Angel Ophlyn

The sanctuary kind of Haven are you, well listen to me Son or Mercidiah and Simeon and pray tell me, what need is there of sanctuary to be called Zyxven, as its very sound is filled with ridiculing preposterous nonsensical egotistical self flattery

Angel Zyxven

Permit me Herald in saying that from the sun and the moon, to the birds and the bees, from the wind and the rain, to the flowers and the trees, from the mountain tops to the valleys beneath, and from the sleepers dreaming of reality, and from the dawn of time to infinity, and from the scripted words of spirituality, and from the wealth of kings to a poor man's creed, and from the cries of birth, til the last breath breathed, I am Zyxven, the sanctuary of Haven

Angel Ophlyn

Zyxven you say?

Angel Zyxven

Yes, Zyxven

Angel Ophlyn

Well then pray tell me young Zyxven, how and what can you from the sanctuary of a choir if not a chorus of Angels, possibly do to defeat a Leviathan

Angel Zyxven

Well in response to that question if you permit me my Herald, it may not be so easy to defeat the Leviathan, other than it may but be possible if you allow me to explain and dictate my methods

Angel Ophlyn

There is no time for the discussions of the dictation of methods, come we must fly now and ascend the skies above at once, before this monster of the sea decides to appetize itself upon your very sanctimonious soul, maybe your methods shall prove to be applicable once we discover and see what we up against

Ext: Angel Zyxven & Stefan Stiles & Angel Ophlyn are instantly united and once again reminded of the hosts of Heaven

Look at these the people of the world and tell me what do you see, for each and every one of them has an angel and guardian host for their own keeping, they are watched over eternally day and night and night through till day, but who watches over them and why indeed do the hosts of heaven themselves need to be of a concern to us, when we in turn watch over them.

Even as a defender of these the realms of humanity even you and I are desired and required to have someone watch over us, although we are not aware of the order of all things that prevail unseen by the living eye, you must remain aware that you are not of the order of the hosts of heaven, you are a defender of it, and so they cannot see you but hear you nor do they truly know of you existence, but bare you, yes there are others like you born into the infinite wars and laws of mankind and their eternal destiny which naturally rests with us and others like us, but your purpose is to serve the hosts the guardians of the Earth, and the will of the realm will concern itself with us, as its' keepers and defender.

If ever uncertain of the way, if ever unsure of the will, and if ever doubtful of the action to take the you must seek out a fellow servant and kindred soul who has the power of knowledge and the understanding to administer it to you in all proportions, and beyond all else to set about equal and fair display of every intention that is made ever present. His soul, his spirit is both young and old and his view is both narrow and short as much as it is wide and longstanding, his name is written as wisdom, and it is written on the hearts and minds of all that is great in human qualities, wisdom is a solitary figure and commands many cherubs in his service, he is nothing but everything all in one breath and sits at the edge of all reasoning, and is also unseen nor can he be found by anyone who is not seeking.

Wisdom is known to frequently habituate as an idyllic proclamation prophesying over the watchtower in this his domain, as a bearer of his foremother and so let it be known that wisdom is only in truth an observer, whose intentions is not to react in the usual regard as the hosts of heaven may appear to do so, nor does he sway with the opinionated revelations of the day or the night or the night through till day.

Regarding the hosts of heaven let it remain with us that if humankind is or are left unguarded for a moment in time, then this is the point that they are not only most vulnerable, but defenseless against Sheol and open to be preyed upon at any point in their natural lives even at an end to the making of their own divisive designs, of course this the cycle of their existence is interwoven with ours and it is this, our predisposition that has linked us to their realm and so the hosts are forever vigilante, and somewhat willingly in all practical portions in our honor and servitude, aware of how to best serve mankind as he is directed through this his natural life.

The more the hosts of heaven can influence and administer to each and every soul, the more the host is able to naturally guide and watch over him, until such appointed time has transpired or come to an end, It is the reason for our being that as defenders not to interfere but to witness, protect and influence in the same natural way as the hosts do and to do all else to guard the realm of heaven itself, In a way we are the intermediary's who purpose is to protect the protector and guard the guardian. The hosts of heaven cannot interfere in this matter nor change the course or destiny of mankind, although we arc also inclined not to interfere in matters unconcerned with us.

This matter has always been considered as the most important relationship between mankind, their guardian angels and us the keepers of this realm simply because mankind and all living beings have a soul which is influenced by a spirit which is naturally influenced by the hosts.

Every host or guardian has a duty to fulfill albeit of a greater or lesser degree to the soul of man, and it is this relationship that is most valued, most sacred and above all else most honored within these realms, only in the depths of the abyss and the dwelling place of the un-living do we exchange one for the other when the soul is released and the spirit is renewed or united with the host.

It is only Sheol that we all watch, wait and look out for eternally, both coming and going in a motion unknown to any of its' kind, as every one of mankind when faced with this, the Angel of Sheol is not aware that the hosts of heaven or his guardian has already prepared and made an agreement in exchange in this the grace of his soul.

Ext: Upon their arrival and their decent upon the place known as Godstone Cemetery, they immediately witnessed and came face to face with the violently enraged and yet somewhat restrained Leviathan but by their arrival and presence, it instantly reacted in an attempt to free and to unleash itself, whilst becoming poised and attracted and drawn to the scent of Angel Stefan.

Stefan Stiles

But how does it know me, it truly knows me, but how can this be?

Angel Ophlyn

Keep back and keep your distance Stefan, for one vicious attack from this beast and you will be no more

Angel Zyxven

Wait, wait Stefan, do not fly for it will out run you

Stefan Stiles

Then what must I do, for I can sense and feel its own will towards me?

Angel Ophlyn

Then we must act and move quickly before it, and what I must do, I must distract and draw it away from you, now be still Stefan and be quick Zyxven and organize apply your methods to this madness

Ext: And so Angel Zyxven continued to recite and speak his words of propheticism from a book known only as the unwritten laws

Angel Zyxven

As to the extent of my understanding of this foe and my knowledge as towards applying the primordial aspects of this beast, is that in principal, nothing can exist outside the laws of creation, except that whatever is determinate as to what can and cannot come into being, also begins with the seclusion of the trinity of one, which then become two, and two becomes three, and then three gives way to the fourth and fifth aspects of the myriad

Angel Ophlyn

Yes! But what must be done Zyxven?

Stefan Stiles

Be quick Zyxven in diluting and weakening this creature

Ext: As Angel Zyxven begins to read from the book of the unwritten laws, Angel Ophlyn descends upon the back of the Leviathan's and attempts to fight and struggle with it, whilst defending Angel Stefan, who by now descends upon the hallowed ground of the cemetery.

Angel Zyxven

The myriad and that of the many things that we come to call and yield into our senses in questioning and beginning with the sixth sense, which is the mark of man and that of the natural senses combined, and then seven which is the virtues of the senses, and then eight which is the laws of the spirit and that of the karma, and then nine which is also the final configuration of that which leads us back to the laws of the universe and that of chaos and order and our very own creation of this Angeldom, which has allowed this Leviathan to evolve and to transgress and arrive upon this plain and dimension of our earthly realm….

Ext: As the embattled Angel Ophlyn was by now struggling to stay astride the back of the Leviathan, as it viciously swung him around tossing him into the air, while attempting to take pursuit after Angel Stefan, even as Angel Zyxven, attempted to keep his wits and focus about himself as he tries to keep his mind upon the reading of the prophetic scriptures.

Stefan Stiles

Zyxven! What must we do, what is this game of numerology that you play, be quick and announce a decree to expel this sea monster

Ext: As Angel Ophlyn attempted to defy the Leviathan by flying and swerving back and forth, using his stealthy advantage to out maneuver this beast of the sea in a roundabout way, so as to also deter and keep it from turning its attention towards Angel Zyxven who was by now somewhat fearfully trembling and shaken with fright by this monstrous beast of the sea, but still somehow he managed to continue reading passages from a book that was once referred to as the unwritten laws.

Angel Zyxven

Although anything pertaining to be considered as that only proven to be worthy of a miracle, as set down and recorded by Pablo Establo Estebhan Augustus Diablo the Immortal One, that could not be consistently verified or confirmed as having any comparison in connection to any other events of this or that kind, could only be deemed as a direct act and intervention of God

Ext: Just then Angel Ophlyn notices and recognizes in identifying and realizing that this ghostly apparition that is hovering over the burial chamber of Selah's gravestone and burial chamber, was none other than that of Hark the Herald Angel, and so to take effect from the immediate opportunity of this sign, Angel Ophlyn beckons to appeal to Hark through his primordial senses to aid him and to instruct him to do his bidding.

Angel Ophlyn

Hark! Pray and listen and take heed after me, for when this act of finality is over and done then we shall once and for all settle this score, but as for now follow my instructions in order for the heavens to act and move against the earth, bring forth and prepare four male lions from their pride in the plains of the wildest wilderness reared in readiness to feed upon the flesh and caucus of this soon to be smitten Leviathan, for once I have discovered its' weaknesses it shall be so, for if it lives and is permitted to escape back to the waters of the abyss from whence it came, then surely once again it will gather strength and momentum and rise up again, and so I count on you my friend to not let it be so

Ext: And so it was that the apparition was no more to be seen, except that as Hark the Herald Angel neared a part of the City and descended over the skies of Nejeru, which was still very much under the development and construction much upon the appointment and due to the fulfillment of the glorification and the edification of the Saints and the Prophets who were deemed to be found in having a determinate agreement, that had once upon a time long, long ago, become preached and prophesied of its own revelation and restoration in the reorganization of all the many nations, that he the one who went in search of rounding up the four Lions as initially instructed him to do so by Ophlyn the Herald Angel, who was once upon a time seen as a friend and a fellow servant of the realm of the Angels of the Abode of the Empyreans, had now once again appealed to Hark the Herald Angel to carry out and maintain such a bidding.

Ext: As it was believed and understood by Hark the Herald Angel that the leaders of the world through the Qonshushmigns and the Elders of the several worlds would work and strive together towards this progress in building and creating a manifesto of unification under the banner of love towards all peoples of this brave and yet fragile ideology that may or may not be interpreted as a faithful and worthy idea, in representing an ideal that one in all could truly accept and sincerely identify with, as such was the task set before them to search and find a redeemable consensus in forgiving the bygone era of the past in setting a new precedence and prevail upon a new course in not only the history but also in the legacy of what it is that defines a world.

Ext: As it was somehow believed by those whom felt or thought that they along with that which was echoed throughout the scriptures, that of those who were deemed to become as ascribed to and identified as the faithfully exalted and exonerated ones as of righteous believers, and of those of whom were to exceed after this trial and battle had come to an end of certainty, in becoming proved that a new chapter would be pronounced and delivered up to this new place providing and pertaining that all the tenets of the scripture were fulfilled, although some skeptics and those of whom were found to have some doubts and reservations in their observations that history would repeat again and again, in believing that time would be unceasing in its' perseverance to return and bring us back to a time of simplicity and yet impractical methods of unconventional and unconstitutionally contradicting ideas of that of the future past, in that we had created and maintained and grown from within, would eventually have to be abandoned if we were to truly formalize a new beginning in proclaiming the reconstruction and resurrected Holy City of Nejeru.

Ext: Now as much as Man has his own free will to choose and to decide his own destiny, it is very much so that between the realms of the Angels of the Abode which is also the Empyreans, and that which is of the Animal Kingdom who were somewhat default and devoid of such a will that is free, which was not made permittable to be assigned and attributed to them, as the Angels were made to be the select intermediaries between God and Man, as much as the animals that live and dwell and graze upon the land and in the wild, are also obedient to the laws of heavens nature, and so it was upon that primordial instinct of a progression toward a universal accord that Angel Ophlyn had bidded the spirit of Angel Hark to go out from this place and round up the heads of the pride of four select Male Lions, and to go forth and harness and bridle and fasten them together to a symbolic chariot and cause the heavens to act and to move over Godstone Cemetery.

Ext: At this point in time Angel Zyxven had come across an important piece of the prophetic scripture outlined in the book known only as the unwritten laws.

Angel Zyxven

Wait a minute, wait a minute I have it, I have it now, it says here in order to secure Stefan's safety and in keeping the Leviathan at bay, at first we must draw upon this hallowed ground, the diagram of circle with a pentagram inside it and then we must mark out the number six three times within the inner circle, and then we must mark out the number seven four times outside the circle, as this will prevent the Leviathan from breaching the inner circle where Stefan must also firmly stand inside of it, and then I must pay heed to begin to exorcise and bind and expel its Angelic flesh in order to weaken its defense, and then it can be defeated of its evil possession in seeking to destroy Stefan, as for the rest of the task I shall leave that to you Ophlyn to wrestle and subdue and render this sea monster incapable and useless

Ext: And so this spoken recitation followed and pronounced its' way from Angel Zyxven lips in order to protect and safeguard Angel Stefan, and yet still the newly elected and reborn and raised and restored to his former glory Angel Ophlyn Herald to the Empyreans fought relentlessly with an unyielding passion unbowed by the rage and ravages of the Leviathan, which between the two of them were both striking endless blow after blow, and attacking and exchanging might after might, locked within an ensuing battle to defeat and gain advantage over one another.

Stefan Stiles

So that's your plan, to plant me in a circle of numbers like a sitting duck and hope that this thing with some magical diagram, doesn't somehow manage or find a way to penetrate, or to break through this invisible wall of protection to get me, I mean can we really believe that, I mean why can't I just get stuck into fighting this thing with Ophlyn and get the job done?

Angel Zyxven

Because it is not written or directed to be explained so, remember Stefan part of this thing is you, I mean imagine for one second that you were fighting yourself and knowing that all of your weaknesses could be used against you, imagine knowing that your own lifeforce could be reversed against you, I mean this thing is you nemesis, your demon, your spiritual adversary, and what's more it's your worst nightmare, and it wants you and needs you more than you truly realize

Angel Ophlyn

Stefan listen good and pay heed to Zyxven, for if you are defeated and consumed by this thing, then it shall gain momentum to threaten us all

Stefan Stiles

Okay I get it, I get it, where do you want or need me to stand
Zyxven?

Angel Zyxven

Just stand in the centre of the pentagram
and I shall do the rest to protect you

**Ext: And so it was that between all the heavens of the earth,
the abode of the Empyreans, and the Celestial abode of the
heavens which all serve to constitute and make up the external
materials of the cosmos and the universe, as it is that through this
metaphysical fabric or very essence of life and those instrumental
parts that come together to give magnitude and depth to the
lifeforce which is also at the very core of our being, inasmuch that
it would seek to make and to have a long and lasting and fulfilling
commitment of union with us at the very least of our truest nature
in understanding and accepting it to be so, as such is our resistance
in believing it to be, that these unknown realities of that which we
take from it in our own existence, also finds us less than willing to
return to it, and for that much which it has given to us contained
in its' unending source of unconditional and yet exceptional
abundance of resource, and so what is it that we take from it if not
love for life, and what is it that we need from it if not life for love, as
such is the apparent truth of the Angel of Justice and the Angel of
Mercy who come to administer to the truth behind our dogmatic
affairs in bringing together the unique and delicate facets of our
love and life, and yet to do so fairly is simply for it to be passed
unto us all through these vestiges of a justices and of a mercy
fulfilled.**

Ext: And yet we in ourselves were less than willing to give to it that much resource in return, when in truth we have taken from it albeit unknowingly, for where is our justice if we are not to be judged, and where is our mercy if we are without appeasement to satisfy such judgments, and so all things must return to from whence they came in order for the judgments of appeasement to be made and satisfied in the name of the Angel of Justice and the Angel of Mercy, which are also to be written down and fulfilled within their experiences and testaments of their acts, and so as it was, Angel Zyxven continued to recite and to speak from the book known as and referred to only as the unwritten laws in an effort to exorcise and to cast out the somewhat aggravated and aggressive sea monster the Leviathan.

Angel Zyxven

For he that has said get thee behind me Satan, has no knowledge of this except other than through his or her own merits of faith, as for the disciples of the bright and morning star, they have many guises upon with which to escape this inevitable fate, as we must all one day come face to face with the reckoning day and hour of our own destiny, and so for those of us who have also said to one to another, what will, or shall we pronounce to say to Adonai upon the day of judgement, that is to say, that even if we are to presented with an opportunity to come face to face before God's good grace, to give such an account of ourselves in such perilous and treacherous circumstances, in order to be deemed worthy and made wholly acceptable in his inextinguishable love for us, say nothing, for your hearts have already jumped forth from your mouths, and your ways have already been declared, and your decisions and destiny, and your words have already resounded within the Heavens, and your way is already laid straight before you, and for your sake, never say never, and yet never is said, and yet never was there once nothing, and yet everything once was, and so too do we say, Thy will be done, and yet all remains undone, and so too do we say, so shall it be written and so shall it be done, and yet still the truth remains the same, as it once was, and now the breadth and the depth, is upon the singularity of our own being, in being instrumental upon the heads of the Trinity and all held in the Eternity of their own occupation in the Seclusion of 111.

Ext: And so the prophetic scriptures were read out aloud by Angel Zyxven with Stefan Stiles the Earth Angel standing firmly within the pentagram of the circle, and so too did the Leviathan begin to release and let out moans and cries of tormented agony in anguish along with the symptoms of excruciating pain, as specs of light began leaping from its scaly skin, and as sparks began leaping from its reptilian layer, as by now the words which Angel Zyxven had read, began to penetrate and have a detrimental and impacting infectious consequence of tearing away and bringing harm to the Angelic substance that was once embedded and contained and now becoming released and freed from the Leviathans body, as by now it began to stagger and weaken and wane in its' advance towards Angel Zyxven and Stefan Stiles, as it also began to hemorrhage with blood bleeding from its' salvinating mouth, but still far from being completely defeated, it would seem that this sea monster from the abyss of the deep would attempt once more to become airborne in order to escape its' ill fated fall towards judgment of execution now prevailing and certainly awaiting condemnation, as also within this midst of this struggle Angel Ophlyn reiterated his prophetic words of commandment towards Angel Zyxven.

Angel Ophlyn

Do not let it escape, for if it lives and is permitted to return back to the waters of the abyss from whence it came, then surely once again it will gather strength and momentum and rise up again

Ext: At this point in time Angel Zyxven felt and knew that this act of finality would somehow indeed have far reaching consequences and implications in bringing about some closure and resolve to the fulfillment of the prophesied scripture and the prophecy and fate of mankind surrounding and concerning the Armageddon of the world, if indeed the earthly angels were to take up their responsibilities and duty that would eventually fall upon their unwavering commitment to the heavens of the empyreans, as it could and would only lead them to victory in their noble integrity in recognition of those that were elected and chosen to stand in its place to be the redeeming Qonshushmigns of the sentient's of mankind, but as it was that this glorifying insight was still somewhat partially doubtful and clouded in mystery, as it was overshadowed by those who were amongst the elders of the hierarchy and the heavens of Nejeru who above all knew and understood that they could overrule this outcome, and so it was that the rest of the whole of this prophecy concerning humanity's day of reckoning, which was still very much foreseen much more before and beyond the prophesied slaying of the Leviathan, but before Angel Zyxven in his representation and defense of the sanctuary of Haven could finish exorcising and reciting the remaining verses of the scripted chapters of the book once referred to and known only as the unwritten laws, the Leviathan in its' recoiling released a venomous amount of sulphur from its' mouth overpowering Angel Zyxven and rendering him unconscious now leaving Angel Stefan out in the open and somewhat defenseless as he stood in the centre of the pentagram.

Ext: And so as the battle unending continued with Angel Ophlyn the restored Herald to the Empyreans, who was by now somewhat beginning to weaken and tire from his tumultuous ordeal, but within this hour of need so too did the Angel of Mercy and the Angel of Justice come to appear within the skies over Godstone Cemetery, to lend a hand in assisting and helping the battered and beleaguered and partially broken and torn Herald in his ordeal come to aid and to assist him at his side, as so to do did the Angel of Mercy begin to attend to the unconscious Angel Zyxven, and so Stefan would have to stand firmly alone in the confidence that the deadly Leviathan would not attempt to come to devour him as the battle ensued.

Ext: As for the strength and the might of the Leviathan and whether it had or really or truly possessed, or knew or felt or resounded with any real and tangible amount of content in its' being, having become aligned to that or if any traits of an enlightened and prolific amount of Angelic substance, or indeed whether within its somewhat prehistoric biology whether it even possessed any real substance of virtue or purity in its form if to desire to know where it had sprung and evolved and come from, or even whether on the surface of all things as they appeared to be whether it was quite simply just a cold blooded winged giant serpent that was quite primitive within its ordinary and basic instincts of being a bloodthirsty creature, with an appetite for Angelic flesh, blood and bone in seeking out that which gave it the ability with which to wreak havoc and destruction in its' wake, as the very core of its' primal nature could only be described and compared to that of a carnivorous dinosaur that had simply come to be, because of the fact that it had indeed nurtured and tasted and feasted upon the decaying spawn of an Angelic seed and so turning towards the Angel of Mercy fearful that Angel Zyxven would also become harmed, and wounded or lost, Stefan calls out to the Angel of Mercy for help and assistance.

Angel Stefan

Do not worry or be concerned after me Angel of Mercy, for you must draw you attentions and turn towards Angel Zyxven, for this reason and purpose I am now duly guarded and protected away from the Leviathan, look away now for it cannot harm or attack me, so be quick and revive him, so that he may finish the exorcism

Ext: And so the Angel of Mercy turned her efforts towards attending to Angel Zyxven who lay upon the ground unconscious, and so she begun by embracing him and pressing her tender lips up against his and began by kissing him ever so gently, whilst releasing a sigh of ethereal breath into his mouth arousing him back to a state of consciousness.

Angel Of Mercy

No way shall it be that my judgment shall proceed to go out and leave and depart before me

Ext; And so it was that when all seemed lost that a chariot being pulled by four Lions did also appear in the skies overhead with Hark the Herald Angel pulling and steering upon its' reigns, as by now the Leviathan had come face to face with Angel Stefan, and as it was about to set and seize upon him by attempting to smoulder and paralyze and suffocate him with its' breath of acidic sulphur, as much as this beast of a sea monster was getting closer and closer to capturing its' intended prey and victim, it would seem that, as it had tried to do so somehow its attack and advance was shielded and deflected away from the powers of the inner circle where Stefan stood, and so it was that Angel Zyxven had resumed consciousness after being affectionately held and kissed by the Angel of Mercy, as also was the defiant Leviathan now becoming tamed and brought down to bow before the Angel of Justice by the hand and the might and the strength and the courage of Ophlyn the Herald Angel, and so it was to be, that the Angel of Justice loftily swung forth her blade in the name of Law and Order, and cut across the neck of the sea monster Leviathan and broke and severed its head, decapitating it away from its body.

Ext: As by now the last few remaining verses of the prophesied scriptures could be heard coming from above on high as Hark the Herald Angel descended upon the hallowed ground of Godstone Cemetery within his chariot, as if by some transcending form of magic or mysticism the Leviathan was unable to breach this invisible wall that had become a protective blanket over Stefan, for it was Hark the Herald Angel himself that had spoken the last few remaining words that were prophesied from the scripture in the midst of this tragic and desperate situation and event, that would prove to be crucial in preventing the Leviathan from achieving its aim and objective.

Hark the Herald Angel

For he laid hold of the Dragon that Serpent of old, who is the Devil and Satan and bound him for a thousand years and cast him into the bottomless pit and shut up him and set a seal on him so that he should deceive the nations no more, from the pit of the Abyss came forth the Serpent of old Satan, as he arrived and made his presence known amongst the Saints and the Prophets and the entire household of Heaven, who were there to bear witness to the trial of the Dragon Devil Satan, and they gathered them together to the place called in Hebrew Armageddon, who is a liar but he who denies that Jesus is Christ he is Antichrist who denies the Father the Son, for many deceivers have gone out into the world who do not confess Jesus Christ is coming in the flesh, this is a deceiver and an antichrist, they shall no more offer their sacrifices to demons after whom they have played the harlot, this shall be a statue forever for them throughout the generations, They sacrificed to demons not to God, to God's they did not know, to new God's new arrivals that your Father did not fear, if Satan cast our Satan he is divided against himself, how then will his Kingdom stand, lest Satan should take advantage of us, when we are not ignorant of his devices.

Ext: And so it was that after the headless body of the decapitated Leviathan was by now fallen and laid down to bare and strewn out and in and amongst the devastation of the dilapidated and derelict Godstone Cemetery now defeated by Ophlyn the Herald Angel, and also by the helping hand of the Angel of Justice who delivered the deciding and final fatal blow in this act of finality, it was finally left to Hark the Herald Angel to unbridle and unfasten the four fierce and ferocious Lions now under his charge and primal instinctive influence from the wilderness, for them to be set free and loosened to feed upon the fleshy carcass of the Leviathan, and to feast upon its' scaly body and to crush and to grind upon its' bones and to extinguish the remains of this sea monster.

Hark the Herald Angel

You look terrible after your eventful ordeal my friend, but pray tell me are you hurt in any shape or form?

Angel Ophlyn

I have fought vicious and vile things before, and this event makes no difference to me although my wings, they are torn and tired to say the least, but I pray and know that they shall heal in time

Hark the Herald Angel

You have done and proved and performed a mighty task my friend, but pray come tell me now what unfinished business did you not come to pronounce to announce to me this day of our Lord God

Angel Ophlyn

Hark, Hark, Hark forever found to be amongst the faithful, and true and trusted servant and friend, as true and as sincere as your name permits you to be, like a song that is sung throughout the heavens of the empyreans, our business is finished, for you did seek to attend to my bidding without question and with neither judgment nor contempt nor distrust or spite and feeling of hate nor anger, and in rescuing my life from destruction, let me declare in saying that these bygone vengeances of yesteryear are bygones and a torment of revenge no more, for I am not now as I once was

Hark the Herald Angel

Then you are redeemed of your ways and your former self my friend is it not?

Angel Ophlyn

Yes it is true, I am new and I also have a dream with which I am promised to fulfill

Hark the Herald Angel

Say nothing, for it was written in the stars that a renewal of the heavens of the empyreans shall soon come to take place, and then soon we shall fly once again together, side by side, Hark and Ophlyn the heralds of angels

Angel Ophlyn

Yes Hark, once again we shall fly through the tetra valley and beyond the realms of Sheol for skies are destined for us

Hark the Herald Angel

Well then my friend, you are most welcome to return to your place amongst the empyreans of Nejeru, and you shall be welcomed back into the flock and the Legions of Angels but not as you are, but as an ordained Herald restored to proper glory, now go Godspeed and become well, for I am certain that one awaits for you

Ext: And so it was that Stefan Stiles was protected and saved from the savage ravages and lethal destruction of the Leviathan, as also was Angel Zyxven somewhat relieved and contented that not only had his life been spared, but also the life of his fellow empyreans were also saved from the chaos of this sea monster, as for Hark the Herald Angel, he continued to supervise and to watch over the four Lions under his charge and command so that no stone was left unturned in the removal of any foreign materials and matter of pollution that could be left over by the previous course of this event concerning the sea monster Leviathan, as these four Lions in particular would also eventually turn out to be unable to be returned to their natural habitat amongst the wilderness, as they too would soon have to come to ascend to play an active part in bearing the face of the four living creatures that were also found to be possessing wings and to become unceasing in their praiseworthy worship in saying both day and night, Holy is the Lord God, the Almighty who was and who is, and who is to come, but as for the Angel of Justice and the Angel of Mercy their work and duty here was for now done and complete, but as for Ophlyn the Herald Angel, he was simply tired and worn out as he slumped down and sat amongst the ruins of Godstone Cemetery somewhat dazed and confused, and yet in a contemplative and melancholic and reflective mood of somewhat mixed emotions, as within his bewilderment of long lasting sorrow and disorientation, and within the thoughts that rested wearily upon his heart and mind of his inner feelings, which somewhat borderlined upon the loss of and the remembrance of his Son Ruen.

Ext: Just then the Angel of Mercy turns to the Angel of Justice.

Angel Of Mercy

My Sister you have slain the beast, this creature the Leviathan that has threatened us all and the heavens above

Angel Of Justice

Yes my Sister it is true the beast is now dead, but even unto you, you have been extra forceful and diligent and courageous in your ways saving the Haven of our sanctuary

Angel Of Mercy

Well then it is done, and we must prevail to leave things as they are attended to by the empyreans, for we have already played our part in cementing our allegiances with them, and for this they shall be forever grateful in holding us in their highest esteem and debt

Ext: At this point Stefan steps from out of the protective circled pentagram that kept him safe and held him in good stead.

Angel Stefan

But pray tell me Angel of Mercy, how is it that you should learn to find and to seek of us here, as we are most fortunate and well and good to see that you have come to our aid and rescue in this hour of need

Ext: The Angel of Mercy begins to laugh to herself.

Angel Of Mercy

How, well how does the Moon influence the seas beneath its' orbit, and how do the seasons know when it is time to change Son of Hark, as it is a question that us most profound to my ears, I mean after all how does anything know of its' own construct and nature, we know simply because it is our business of interest to know and to also keep vigil and watch for such an event, for it were not the sign of the pentagram in which you stood, then as it is prophesied and proclaimed that the one who would seek to threaten and tear down the heavens and cause the skies to fall beneath our celestial birthplace, might also have appeared here within this forsaken place, and so we have come and appeared as it is written before you this day, so that we might hasten to smite him also along with this Leviathan

Angel Zyxven

Mercy, I am glad for you and I am honored and enamored by your graciousness with great respect and admiration, for you have prevented my destruction and saved me and the life of Stefan from certain death

Angel Of Mercy

I too am happy that your spirit is most fortunate and gladdened my Haven, and who knows perhaps one day or one aeon from now, no doubt you shall come to return the favor and do the same for me

Angel Zyxven

No doubt I shall be most glad and willing to do you such a service Angel Mercy, and I shall keep my deepest and sincerest admiration and faith in you always

Angel Of Mercy

Then I bid thee farewell, now come my Sister, for we must fly high over yonder and seek out destiny toward that which is the abode of our celestial heavenly home.

Ext: And with that farewell the Angel of Justice and the Angel of Mercy took to the skies once again homeward bound to the Celestial Abode.

Ext: But where does the flight of an Angel begin, or is it simply because the flight of an Angel is not just simply a flight beginning from one place to another, or for an Angel to simply go out from the places of their ascent and departure, so as to reach some point in time aligned to a predestination perhaps, for where is an Angel destined to fly to if not to their heavenly home, for the flight of an Angel is filled with that substance of an awe inspiring amazement, of both will and transcendence, simply born to navigate the stars and the elements within from one world to the next, and so it was that Ophlyn the newly transformed Herald Angel was by now somewhat weary and disenchanted and deeply troubled from battle, and was by now ready and prepared to once again take flight within the skies, now flying and soaring into and beyond the vast spaces above him with a renewed spirit of conviction and vigor coupled with a deep desire for love and passion, as by now he was somewhat stealthily guided by his torn and slightly broken wings which still somehow guided him further and further into the skies above, until finally all at once he is out of sight and out of view disappearing into the blackened deep blue beyond, high above the stratosphere until nothing but the clouds beneath him now begin to stir and darken gradually blocking out the Suns fading intermittent rays of light, occasionally breaking through until a storm begins to awaken, now rumbling with the echoes of thunder as the arising winds bring little comfort to such a tortured soul in the aftermath of such an onslaught.

Ext: Just then Stefan turns to his father Hark the Herald Angel.

Stefan Stiles

Once again my father it is good to see you upon this day of judgment and upon this day in paradise, and I trust and pray that all is well with you upon this hour?

Hark the Herald Angel

Stefan my son, my wonderful son, born of me and my beloved Selah, always full of pleasurable awe, excitement and amazement, but pray tell me Stefan, did you not fully understand or grasp in coming to know that before you were born, that my spirit did indeed yield unto you even as you were not yet only a child but also as a new born infant, but now that you have grown and matured into the beautiful creation of the heavens, I must now take this opportunity to reveal to you, that it is time now that you must also yield unto the spirit for all things to become complete in you amongst the Legions of your fellow empyreans

Stefan Stiles

But what does that mean father?

Hark the Herald Angel

It means that you have completed your covenant with God, and for that reason and purpose your timespell shall one day come to expire

Stefan Stiles

My timespell, but what do you mean, expire, when, how, why?

Hark the Herald Angel

I do not know the day or the hour Stefan, for only you shall know when it is time, perhaps only as of when you are most enlightened and prepared to yield once again unto your spirit or even unto me, for all things must return to from whence they came, as much as I am one day bound to also be called unto the salvation of my own yielding unto the creator of all things in this world and the next

Stefan Stiles

But by what authority and what power is this to be father, and how can this be, is it true?

Hark the Herald Angel

It is only by the powers of the most high that through these manifestations of spirit and soul, that we are all called into the service of that which we shall all come to question, and yet so it is written then so shall it be done

Stefan Stiles

Then by thy will, how will this be done father?

Hark the Herald Angel

It is only by the act and the will of faith that all these things shall come to pass, for all of that which is done is, must also one day be undone my son

Stefan Stiles

Then I shall one day see you when my dreams are no more

Hark the Herald

Yes one day we shall see each other for the last time

Ext: And within that moment Stefan become somewhat melancholy and thoughtful and yet saddened by the news that his father Hark the Herald Angel had revealed and imparted to him.

Ext Zyxven

Ext: And all of a sudden the full revelation was revealed to Angel Zyxven, as it was once said that to enter the kingdom of heaven, that we must first become like children, and now even in this moment he no longer felt for the need of things that he would be able to put in accordance with the world at large, as it was all but a stream of consciousness flowing eternally through time, and yet it was even said, that the kingdom of heaven could be found in a grain of sand and yet we seek it within if only to contain it, but we have never found it in ourselves to walk along a sea swept sandy beach thinking and feeling that this heaven could be forming its' foundation beneath our feet, as no one could see that they were indeed already within this place.

Ext: And as his memories flooded in and became more incensed with the absolute, he began to recall upon his own tumultuous experiences, in recalling that so it was, that once upon time in the abode of the heavens lived an Angel known only as Pablo Establo Estebhan Augustus Diablo or simply Pablo the Immortal One, and as it was prophesied that he should be the keeper of the seal of the unwritten laws and serves as a witness of the probable outcome and determinate fate of mankind and humanity between the heavens and the earth and all the realms and dominions in the life thereafter.

Ext: And it was upon his recounting of this memory that Angel Zyxven realized that it was Pablo the Immortal One, who was the stranger in and amongst the Elders of the Several Worlds, and that somehow it was he that had handed him the book known only as the unwritten laws, as it was also at such a time when he began to feel very tense and fearfully panicked, as if he as the Angel Haven of the Sanctuary, and in becoming the Sanctuary of Angel Zyxven, had merged into one uniting force, in realizing that his presence occupied more than one place or position in time, causing a swift and chain reaction within the elements of this new development, which would bring about this God divine creation of a New Heaven and a New Earth, but not before revealing to Angel Zyxven upon his departure, a book that was somewhat obscured with familiarity, and that which Pablo had handed to him upon the simple instruction that he should replace or quite simply put the book back and return it to from whence it came, and with that remark Pablo had vanished and disembarked leaving Angel Haven or indeed Angel Zyxven within the becoming advancement of his own trial.

Ext: And so it was that upon reflection and the second sight of seeing an alternative reality now becoming revealed or presenting itself to Angel Zyxven, in the event of being faced with a life threatening experience, it had dawned upon him, that after coming across an account of things that were very much left open to his interpretation as noted and set down by Pablo Establo Estebhan Augustus Diablo the Immortal One, was that a plan, or indeed a developing construction of reality was taking shape and unfolding and even as in the pretext of the events that had come and brought them all here in defense of Angel Stefan, so it was to be that Angel Zyxven along with this depth of insight and knowledge that was contained in the book of the unwritten laws, had now begun drawing upon his own connection and the comparisons of the same revelations that were originally cited as the coming forth of the New Nejeru, and that of The Other Place that had once been proclaimed in his own name as being the Sanctuary of Heaven, which was also above and beyond the same place where the Six depths of Hell had also indeed indicated and given over to the Seven highs of Heaven, whereupon those who were indeed saved by this act of authority, had by now been led away, which left Angel Zyxven to believe and to comprehend that all in all, a transformation was already taking shape and effect by the very nature and the very acts and the very presence of all these Angels everywhere simultaneously, fulfilling the scriptures of the unwritten laws and in bringing about and realizing that the other place was in fact the New World .

Ext: And so it was that as they all remained conscious and reflective of their ordeal with the Leviathan, and then suddenly all around everything became and fell silent about them, as if a cold chill had come about in the air, and so it was that a star twinkling and glistening from up above did begin to draw near and come forth from out of the embodiment and from within the Heavens, and as it did it began to take shape and form, as it began descending there upon the place where they all gathered together in Godstone Cemetery amongst the ruins and the aftermath of the battle which had by now come to an end, and so it was that from out of this starlight of all luminosity and illumination, did a very distinctive Angel step through and come forth and forward from within a disc of light, and did appear to have about it a gracious presence in bearing a disc of light that was set about and shone brightly above and upon and from behind its head, and so it was that this Angel in its observations seemed to take in all and everything that was around and about it, and as it did so, it spoke very softly in saying.

Angel Aura

Show me something that you have not yet seen, and tell me something that you were not yet told, and explain to me the truth of reality concerning all things, and speak to me of things that you have never known

Hark the Herald Angel

But how is this possible, and who and what are you friend or foe?

Angel Aura

Silence Hark, for I neither friend nor foe, and for which I am the discipline of the disciples, and I am the obedience of those who obey, for it does not abode nor permit me to hear you speak

Angel Of Justice

But what kind of unfair questions are these my fair and beautiful one, and from where do you descend to inquire after such examination?

Angel Aura

Silence Justice! For I am the sentient and the beneficent Aura of all living things, and these are not simply merely the questions of examination inasmuch that they are the will and the unanswerable voices of God

Angel Ophlyn

The voices of God! But who and what are you, and for what reason and for purpose has he sent you to us, and why do you seek to speak to us and to address us with such confounded questions of riddle and ridicule?

Angel Aura

Hold your tongue Ophlyn, for I am the Aura of the Halo, and it has taken charge of me to administer and to ordain unto each of you whom are present, with such a gift of God, for as it is through him that what is established upon the firmament is also established upon the Earth, and once the foundation is set, then there is naught else to be done except that all things take effect and arise from out of such an established foundation

Angel Zyxven

A gift from the Most High you say, but what kind of gift exactly is it, and for what merit and purpose?

Angel Aura

Be silent Zyxven, for it is permitted and granted to me to bestow upon all of you, the gift of Absolution

Ext: Stefan becomes confused

Stefan Stiles

Absolution! Eternity! Immortality for us, but how is this so, and wherefore shall we dwell upon receiving such a gift from the Angel of the Aura if we are not to be found residing within our Heavenly home,

Angel Aura

You shall dwell within the same time and occupy the same space that I too also reside and occupy within

Ext: And so it was that the Angel Aura did indeed administer and bless them all one by one, in bestowing upon there being the same disc of light that it did indeed also possess itself above and behind and upon its' own head, and so it was that this disc of light was now to be placed above and upon all of their heads, which was that of the heads of the Angels of Empyreans and also that of the Angels of the Celestial Abode, as it was that this light that had come to represent the Absolution of all Creation, Eternity and Future of both Past and Present, then so too did it also now come to hold and support and sustain itself as a disc of light upon their being and behind and above their heads, and so it was that as this act of Absolution was fulfilled and performed, that it was to be through this act and this blessing, that they all would receive the Aura through the light and the Halo of all luminosity and illumination which had now been bestowed upon all of them by this Angel, who upon completion of her duties, had by now already begun to take leave and to depart from this place in Godstone Cemetery, and so it was that this disc of light that was above and upon the head of the Angel Aura began to excite and to flare and to brighten so intensely, that it expanded and glowed. whilst increasingly growing and consuming her entire celestial body, as the act of Absolution was now complete and fulfilled, and so it was that this departing Angel and messenger was by now ascending and becoming further and further away, until seemingly so, it became so far away in the distance, that it just appeared to hang and shine in the heavens amongst the stars simply only appearing to be no more significant than the other stars that were grouped there around it, as if it were merely only a shining crystal high above Godstone Cemetery.

Int: In preparation to be ready and to begin her consummation with the one with whom she had readily and freely chosen to give her mind and her heart to, and to eternally share the breath and the embodiment of her soul with, Kali Ma chose to wash her hair with the essences of almonds, and to cleanse her body from head to toe in argan oil, whilst happily chanting and praying to make her invocations firm and sincere, as well as to sincerely remain pure and true, for as much as she is an Earth Mother of virtue and one who is also blessed and gifted with a spiritual nature and insight in notably being able to see beyond the secrets of the unknown, as it was for her that with each droplet of water, that she was to bathes herself with only simply to purify her mind and soul in this way so as to be ready for the event in receiving her beloved Ophlyn by her side, as for Kali Ma herself it is simply and only because no man of any means or considerations has ever seen beneath her veil of natural beauty, and so it was that after her ablution and self vows were made, that she set beside her bed a clock to welcome in the hour that he was to return, as she now felt that she was ready for this act of consent to take place, and as for now she had made herself ready to satisfy and to fulfill her promise to him, which was to submit and to yield unto Ophlyn the Herald Angel a Son of good intent and great virtue, and so soon the time was drawing near that another dream of the Angel babies would come to begin, and upon his creation he shall come to be heralded in as a hero and a warrior as of the Nephilites from the days of yore, if only notably for the consequences of man in his comings and goings, had already advanced himself much more beyond his own ways and means in seeking out ways with which having sought to recreate creation.

Int: And so it was that as Kali Ma laid awake relaxing upon her bed listening to the echoes of music in the wind, that the night time had crept in amongst the night air of softening bliss now speaking of true love, and growing and increasing and manifesting in her conscious mind becoming unified with a rhythm now in syncopation to the words and the melody of a song, that only the midnight skies which were alight could hear amongst the stars now beginning to stir up a fever of nocturnal passions keeping her amused and slightly disturbed and restless, as time and sleep begins to beckon away.

Int: As the chiming clock is resting upon a bedside table has been readily adjusted and set to welcome in a new day and a new dawn much before the present day has ended, as Kali Ma lays down with the thought of a prayer which has finally brought her to rest in slumber as she lays down to sleep and is instantly transported and greeted within the realms of dreams upon the eleventh hour, but outside the window the darkening skies are by now becoming agitated by the aggressive insistent winds sailing toward their destiny, as if reaping and sowing destruction upon the unsuspecting households and homes below, but the world outside which was also unaware of the amorous affection growing inside of her and taking root deep in her emotions, born of a love conceived and soon to be received by the recipient that decorates her heart body and mind, as the beside clock chimes away the weary hours now flowing like music through the veins of this dreaming Earth Mother.

Int: And yet beneath a deep subconscious hypnotic surrealist dream, the elements of air, earth, fire and water are brought into contention with one another as the full force of an eventful storm begins by ripping apart the streets and the fabric of familiar structures and objects that give way and meaning to the constructs of an environment or society, uprooting and tossing aside and turning over trees creating mayhem in its wake, whilst blowing yesterdays debris across the lonely winding abandoned streets of an unconscious city, And yet some would say if a Butterfly were to gently flap its' delicately weaved sensitive beautifully decorated wings, that it could indeed send out eternal vibrations across the winds of time and conjure up such mysterious and perpetual violent storms, and still yet hardly disturb these unsuspecting drifters of dreams upon the highways of counting an endless succession of an ever changing, ever evolving world outside so as to enter into the neverland of a never world, and yet the mind is already set upon a course mapped out and charted within the stars above by the elements of a soul mate returning from a trial of tribulations, brought together by their choices of fate and destiny combined, to begin a declaration and to fulfill a contract between the stars that navigate the souls of mankind.

Ext: For if it were not for the birds of the sky to be made nested and silently perched upon the winds of this prevailing storm rooting out their hiding places and sanctuary's within, with nowhere to fly too except toward the place of their own heavenly and spiritual home, for had it not been for the storm in its' relentless enduring pursuit violently and viciously lashing its' aggressive onslaught like an angry whirlwind of a torrent across the mainland, who could have known where they would have flown too, as the dream commenced even ever more deeper, and ever more beyond the depths and the realms of tranquility, where kisses send shivers into tongues as they tingle with the sweet sensuality and the sensation of an aphrodisiac saliva now found to be arousing the senses of taste buds to delight, melting like sweet butter into the mouth of an all authoritarian word that turn into sounds, and that of the sounds that become the moans and groans of a lustfully yearning fed like nectar to the spiritual soul in one sequential moment after the next, whilst the clock never stops to think and to consider of itself in contemplation if indeed it does possess the eternity of an endless eternity.

Ext: Morning drifted in heavily laden and burdened with clouds sailing across the skyline like ghost ships carrying the cargo of battered voyages forever destined to encircle the globe, bringing with it expectations of things anew that immediately remembered as once was the dream that evoked emotions of Butterflies that now stir within the stomachs. Although somewhat accompanied by disjointed palpitations in the stroke of a romantic heartbeat, for as Kali Ma had awoken and arisen from her never world of a never land unharmed and unscathed by the vicious winds of the storm of the night before, still unaware of the chaos and the destruction now living and breathing outside upon the desolate battered plains of another world, with which hastens her to the readiness of fashionably adorning herself with clean garments to match and to compliment Angel Ophlyn, whilst in anticipation of preparing to greet and meet with him upon his return from the devastations and the destruction of the night before.

Ext: A Grey mist hung in the air as the streets now strewn in the aftermath of a worldly blitz, as she awaits attentatively upon the hour if only to see if he will appear to come, and to spend time and to redeem her, even as the morning had begun and then given way to the early afternoon, still not a soul could be seen, and yet a familiar scent hung in the air, known only to one as being scented with perfumed flowers entered in by the window followed by Ophlyn the Herald Angel, as Kali Ma with a spark in her eyes upon receiving him in his appearance, became much more radiant and attractive to her beloved, which brought about the ending of the day in perfect harmony with a contented smile, and a look paid for in a simple glance, and in that moment not a word was spoken, but the contract was fulfilled and filed away, and so once again the evening flowed into the hypnotic hours of a dream for wherever they were, they were together in both space and time a beautiful place.

Ext: For what could the storm claim, and who could the storm claim, and how could the storm claim to be the victor possessing the victory over two hearts such as these, as it was naught else but a storm compared to the love now stirring and brewing beneath the depths of tranquility, born out of the hearts of this Mother of the Earth and this Herald Angel of the Empyreans in need of their unbridled passion to be released like heat bustling and bursting up like eruptions from a fiery furnace in the ground below, as even before this endless moment in time Ophlyn had made his way through the pandemonium and the chaos of dereliction, did at last come to find rest and love and peace of mind, where once there was none, and so for him to be received and welcomed and cared for and embraced in all of his own turmoil's and neediness and vulnerability and triumph, then so it would be that Kali Ma that would be the one to come and to cement and to yield her virtues of Karma and of serenity unto him.

Int: As Ophlyn the Herald Angel finally came to arrive at Kali Ma's beside, her heart was lifted by the sheer magnitude of his presence as his wings were now wide open and ready to receive her into a loving embrace, and so as it was that Ophlyn took her unto his bosom although still somewhat shattered and torn upon his frame from the battle, but still both devotedly and completely wrapped up in each other's encompassing concealment of embrace, and without hesitation and reservation they both began kissing upon contact, and yet no sooner than they did, that Ophlyn' torn wings began to blossom and renew themselves upon his scarred and bruised and battered body, as the more Ophlyn the Herald Angel tightened his deepening embrace around Kali Ma, the more his torment and suffering and pain was being extinguished, penetrating deep beneath their emotions and entering beneath their innermost intentions and feelings that they felt towards one another, with Ophlyn complimenting Kali Ma for echoing love's salvation of gratitude towards him, and yet as they both gently nurtured each other, for now Kali Ma was affectionately satisfied and amused by Angel Ophlyn's strength and passionate nature, which was also complimentary and appealing to her very own nature and character.

Int: As it was in the dark that they both did discover the beating bosom in the art of the pleasurable heart, upon the quest for the unquenchable thirst for the sweat upon the body and the perspiration upon the palms, removing layers upon layers of clothing to expose and reveal the need to want and to touch precious virgin skin, whilst mentally accelerating towards the giddily heights and relief of frustrations and tensions of exhilarations underneath the influence of obsessive desires and acquired infatuations, both madly and frantically trying to indulge in the others sensitivity, whilst exploring the intimate parts of each other's bodily anatomy, and the physical terrain and contours of the human form laid bare astride that of an Angel, kissing and touching and learning how to know each to explore each and every conceivable part of one another's anatomy, tossing and turning to and fro, to move as one both playful in behavior, softly, gently, lovingly and attentatively, and sensuously and tenderly exploring the softly exposed erogenous zones responding to ticklish sensitivity, pressing palm against hand and hand against thighs, whilst sensuously biting the nape of the neck, clutching against the bedstead to steady their sturdy and playful activity, passively fighting for complete ecstasy, empowered with infinite passions, frenzied with an intimacy releasing and contracting their statuesque torso's and then finally yielding to their unspeakable romantic devotional fantasy, until they could struggle no more but learn to nurture the love that they had consumed, and that had led them both to offer and give themselves to each other freely and devotedly.

Nejeru

Angelus Domini

~*~

I   N   R   I

Iesus Nazarenus Rex Iudaeorum

INSPIRIT*ASPIRE*ESPRIT*INSPIRE*

The Angel Babies Nejeru
Angelus Domini

~*~

INSPIRIT*ASPIRE*ESPRIT*INSPIRE

Let us firstly begin with the things that we are all truly aware of and with that with what we can accept as a form of tangible and real evidence as in our understanding of both a conscientious and awareness that brings about a scope of reality, that what we wish to prevail towards or overcome in our commitment towards both God and Heaven, as firstly so that we can all recognize what it is that is fundamentally at the root and universality of all things as in all shape and forms, as in accepting that what we all share and experience in complete uniformity despite where we live and dwell upon the Earth, as it is in our interest and ability in recognizing and also realizing that our common practices and that of our commonplace in alignment and in proximity to one another as to what we can see as the prevailing reality of commonsense, of what we would all identity with as being the sum of all reasoning and totality that we could all agree upon in its acceptance.

As once we have seen and realized this universal accord and furthermore become attuned to it, then we can begin to identify and engage to accept the basic principles behind its' valuable teaching of what it is that is truly to our advantage and potential of what we are attempting to pursue as the beneficial and positive ideals for all concerned, but as for when we realize this universal governing principle, which in truth is also not ours alone, but also in comprehending and realizing that we have already allowed ourselves to rise above and out of its idea and teaching in opening up our minds and eyes to see far beyond this first scope of understanding that with regards to making the first steps towards creating or building a Heaven on Earth with a view towards seeking what it is that we are attempting to establish as a Makepeace union with one another.

Now let us see what is beyond the destruction of the mortal body, which is also that which naturally happens upon its' inevitable separation from the spirited soul, as it is finally left to decay into the Earth, which is also in itself a commonplace activity of phenomena, that can also engage along with nature in allowing itself to become a fertile vessel, through its interconnectedness of blending and teeming with plant and insect life, which also by the way are inevitably fed upon and nourished from such a natural body of decay albeit of a past usage and waste within this vast ecosystem, unless indeed a body is preserved to endure such a succession of years, but still the inevitable consequence of these events are exactly the same and remain the same overtime, as it is also open to the elements of decay, but even in such a delicate and natural way this ecosystem still maintains a regulated method of sustaining life after life, generating enough resource for even the simplest of natures creatures, that even we as humans could learn to accept and rationalize as being, or as becoming an unavoidable truth of nature that somehow stems from a natural event that is easy for us all to identify with, as much as perhaps being the overall balancing and natural order of all things in nature.

Now let us look at the spirited soul that is separated away from its decaying body, for it is a continuation of its former self, as upon its journeying, it must also serve to nourish and to sustain and to replenish itself through the elements within the atmosphere as it seeks in its advances of enduring this transition from one body to the next along within this stratosphere, by being and becoming subject to the laws of the metaphysics and personified nature as it carries the information and the experience and the knowledge of its' own examination and truth, which by now is under the influences of that which it has witnessed within the lifecycle of its' own time, although through its' own progression, it is by now through definition not characterized by its physical destructed body, as unlike the physical body which is deceased, the spirited soul is more abundantly attuned to that of a super body, evolving and metamorphosing, and generating out of its own composition of experience of the world that has fashioned it, in temporarily being its' home and habitat within which it has and for a time been in subjection too for the duration of its' physical life.

Of all the things that are commonplace and common practice concerning the destruction of the body, well no matter where we seem to live or dwell upon the Earth the basic tenets and principle embedded in our beliefs, is that with regard to the spirited soul, is that we all commonly believe or at least widely accept that the spirited soul is transcending above and beyond towards either what we call or refer to as Heaven, or indeed towards another transient place of existence and inhabitance, and so whether we can agree upon the actual resurrection of the physical body is somewhat hard to address and to define by definition as it is difficult to explain in the common sense of our understanding of it, unless the real body is also that of the body that has arisen to be and become the super body which is also that which is the composition of the spirited soul.

As the natural destruction of the physical body is also consistent with the natural progression of the spirited soul, then it is as it stands that we can only reach a state of enlightened emancipation upon the informed intelligences of our own universal awareness through the maturity and fulfillment of our own lives, as much before and somewhat by definition, that even as we begin to exceed and to excel far beyond and much further beyond the present position of our status quo, then so it is that in the event of our experiences, and in the present and current context of our existence, it is only our reality that would suggest and maintain that the lifespan of our temporary but physical bodies, is approximately seventy years or more or less depending on the health and the quality of our present existence, but as for the super body then perhaps we can entertain the idea and the notion that we may come to inherit or to fulfill such a super body, which may be born of an accord that is more attuned to the era of the time, or even perhaps defined by the potential products of our environment, or even perhaps be more consistent with the elements that we are most likely to gravitate towards, or most likely to become aligned too, or most likely even in the event and also perhaps in the reality of our own intuitive behavior patterns, may simply become developed through the basis of our own internal workings and knowledge.

As for the designated destination of the spirited soul, then we should suppose and imagine then, that if it could speak then it would tell us of such a place of destination, and yet then again if it could spell, then surely it would write down such a place of a destination, and yet furthermore if it could clearly see into this place of expectation, then surely it would become revealed and shown to us as such a place of destination, as it is only beyond the emancipation and the release from this world, or indeed to find freedom away from the decay of the physical body, then so it is that the progressive spirited soul of the super body is made ready and prepared to know where it is destined to ascend or to arrive to next, as it is upon its' arising, that it is under a source of or at .least under an influence of intuitive instruction, that can only become revealed when such a spiritual soul has reached such a perfection of maturity.

*ABSOLUTE*INCENSED*

And so it was that alliances were formed and agreements were forged and sealed, as were covenants brought to their fulfilment within the varying degrees of the three Heavens, between the Empyreans, the Celestial Abode and that of the earthly sphere that influenced its' spiritual dictates over mankind. And of all the unspoken acts of the Angels of Man and Humankind who were destined by the will of the Tetragrammaton and that of the Universal Architect, who were called upon once again to return to their Heavenly and Celestial Abode having stood and served in the good faith and stead of God and Man, to once again fulfil a binding oath and contract in being that this would usher in a new age that would also see them through this collective union in giving over their inheritance to the world, and in beginning the process of sustaining and restoring the world back to its' former glory amongst the stars in the universe.

And so for a time the world had remained unguarded and unprotected as a period of transition had begun and was underway, with the changes of rebalancing the appropriate attributes of power from the select elected Angels of the Angeldom, which was now to be transferred and passed along and onto the influence of the Qonshushmigns, as these elected Elders were of those whom were inclined and more surely aware and more assertively to be attuned, as to the will of what new era should come to be proven and to be ushered and summoned in, so as to fulfill the future and indeed the fate of this and them that were of the several worlds, and that of the reality of which was mankind in the making, and of whom would be found to be amongst them to be assuredly affirmed and blessed in such a way so as to govern and to be infinitely inspired so as to fulfill this invisible contract and agreement the laws pertaining to Heaven and that of humanity.

And so from a line of the One Million Seven Hundred and Twenty Eight Thousand Legions Of The One Hundred Forty Four Thousand Angels who were amongst the many of the multitudes that were of the natural order of the Three Heavens of those whom were also pertaining to be the servants of whom they were of the duly elected and made representatives of the prophecy of the Hosts' of Heaven or the indeed the Qonshushmigns, which in its totality amounted to become Twelve Thousand Angels from each Legion who came before the Elders in the several worlds in their service to fulfill the last remaining tenets of the scripture, which was to resurrect and to rebuild and to create the new world, which was also recorded and cited in the passages and the chapters and verses as bearing the name of Nejeru of the new world or the New Jerusalem, which had always been the subconscious seed that the Hosts of Heaven had planned and planted and left overtime as a fruitful seed of recognition in remembrance of restoring and returning the world into the hands of its universal creator.

And so it was that all of these selected Angels of the Three Heavens had divulged and revealed their vast and extensive insights of knowledge and transcendental understanding of experience from the guidance and the influence upon the animate soul and the spiritual nature of man, in revealing that the dream of Angel Babies had now returned from the Earth and was by now quickly to be relayed and planted within the body of the Qonshushmigns in that it would eventually come to lead them to reveal upon the awakening of this revelation the acceptable reality that would in turn prevail to take effect on the whole of humanity and mankind in influencing his will to begin to follow their perfection in bringing this Earthly Kingdom into the realms of God's love and light.

As it is said in Heaven that everything is eternal and cannot nor does not die, and so then what is it to become pronounced amongst all things that are immortally so, for us to be or for us to do, as it may be suffice to say that the Heavens are eternally evolving and transforming itself at will, and so no one singular element of strand of infinite truth of existence is predominantly fixed of finite at any time as being aligned for one to dominant over the other, as all things within the Heavens are constantly changing much out of what has already taken effect or precedence before it, as it is by definition that this will shall cause and effect the ruling or almighty guiding truth of the Heavens albeit upon the Earth, which is also determined by the many stands of variable truths of mankind's experience of influence that has also impacted upon the responses and reflected upon the responsibilities that have resulted in learnt reactions by the very Angels that have watched over and learnt by their protective stance in being aligned to man and becoming ordained to take care of us in their custodial role, as they are very much made to be prepared and ready to watch over us if only for themselves to benefit from holding us in their safekeeping.

As it was during this time and period of transition that pockets of unrest and discontent and conflicts had arisen and broken out across the many lands and territories bringing with it disputes amongst the many various different types of groups and factions in support of their ideas and beliefs of interpretation which very much mirrored what was taking place in the Heavens of how mankind shall proceed to be governed, as such was the world in so much chaos and crisis, that as it echoed throughout the Earth, so too did it begin to spread its destabilising volatility across the lower Heavens at a time when there needed to be an air of influential consensus that would be brought through across the Three Heavens to help mankind govern themselves out of their own destructful and erroneous ways.

And so even as these problems had arisen and come about and divided and escalated into many extreme conflicts, it would seem that many of these campaigns and struggles and fights for the rights of independence and for the advantage of power was somewhat short lived in terms of the time it took for the Angels of the Abode to ally and align themselves alongside the Qonshushmigns, even though the world was under the influence of disillusionment and fear and instability, which also affected the hearts and the minds of the people who were caught up in these struggles, as being those that were either opposed to war, or for those that were desperate to take or seize control towards the autonomous rule of their dictates and ideology over the world.

High above the Earth are the Lower Heavens, which is also followed by the Mid Heavens, which is then in turn followed by Highest Heaven, as the foundation or the Higher Heavens is also the dwelling place of the Tetragrammaton, which is also found within the Highest Heaven, the Highest Heaven is light years or aeons away from both the Mid Heavens and the Lower Heavens, and the Mid Heavens are also light years away from the Lower Heavens, as also the Highest Heaven has dominion and precedes and resides over all the other Heavens combined, as it sets in motion and carries forth the intelligible construction and detailed information of the structure and the outline or the blueprint of all the Heavens unified in that it contains and maintains all that is within its translation and influential and transcendent and relative and yet constituent power that is between the Mid and the Lower Heavens, which is also in itself the initial and primary force of right of way or passage for engaging with the journeying of spirited souls from one world to the next or indeed from the Lower to the Higher Heavens.

As there is only the aforementioned creation of the re-establishing of the world as well as it being written and meditated upon in its prophesying, then it can only begin its true root of inception as a fundamental belief that is taking shape and hold not only in the Heavens but also upon us if not through our experienced and deductive reasoning, which also tells and informs us that so on Earth as it is in Heaven, and so it is with this careful reasoning and meditation that the world upon which we stand is also that which we are seeking, and that which is yet to be realised and raised up from the rocks and stones beneath our feet that is needed to build and to erect such a monumental idea from such a profound dream as of yet to be revealed to the world in its entirety, and so it is by now that through our divine nature and instruction that it rests upon the conscious brow of all those blessed and concerned with the potentiality of not only comprehending the universality of such a dream but also in realising what type of will that we must now assume in order to engage the correct aptitude and level of service needed for understanding what needs to be done in order for the world to complete such a task, as Heaven and Earth are not just simply made up of minds that can interpret such profound truth of conviction in spite of what it is that we believe can or cannot be achieved, but also in believing that with such a mindset of acknowledgment that however challenging things may seem or indeed can be, then we must persist in professing that all things are possible with God.

Before we arrive upon the horizon where the Sun sets upon the Sea in the West, then first let us take stock and awaken with the coming of the new Dawn rising up from the East now issuing forth a New Day, as we must also journey forth toward this eventful horizon in order to meet with its expectation of what it is that we shall come forth to receive and impart upon the fruitful nature of our being, and so as we make inroads so at to take and make pathways and passages as we go in search toward our will of submission in seeking the prized possessions soon to be uncovered and given over to us freely forever yielding up to us from the vast richness and properties of the Earth, as so it is that upon our journeying that we must learn to engage as we break stride and yearn to pursue alternative paths and routes towards the North, so as to hasten the seeking and the finding out of our journeying whilst taking refuge from the higher regions that brings chance and challenges to our ever enduring discoveries filled and with the plentiful nature of the land beneath our feet, for even as we head South in search of prosperity and an abundance of labour in working and restoring the land to our pleasurable advantage, so to must we plant crop and seed to yield over to us its harvest, so as to replenish and sustain our feverish bodies as we once again take strength and sustenance from our firm footing as we seek once again to chase down the eventful road that brings us ever more closer to the edge of the Sea, so as to watch the Sun set upon the sign of our sights of the hour whilst we are dreaming of seeking out the terrain of territories of other worlds, as such is the beckoning horizon that can only suggest to us, that when we are certain of the way, then we shall come to know the Sun that is now setting upon the rising the Star of Nejeru.

When the Elders of the several worlds communicate, it is with patience and practical wisdom of the simple matter found to be arising out of the consciousness of the universe, for the very essence of their respective and timeless thoughtfulness is knowledge personified, for they are not thinking, as they have already thought, and they are not feeling, for they have already felt, but still they are aware that out of the root of the nature of their very being, that they are not realising, for they have already realised, and as they are informed as to whom of what is it that they informing, as it is with such a will of that which is to be done of all things that are to arise and to become arisen, so as to satisfy the arising and perfect gift of imparting that which is true in that which is to rise and to fulfil its' own beginning as being the constituent nature of both Heaven and Earth.

Even as we look forward towards a new time, still we are very much reminiscent and reminded of the all too familiar places of a past that have perhaps come into being much before we truly could establish a concrete understanding of it, as such is the world that Kingdoms have risen and Kingdoms have fallen throughout the histories of time, but it is not the legacy nor the history of Kingdoms that have once become risen and fallen as once proclaimed by the prophets and soothsayers of their time, as the Qonshushmigns and the Hosts of Heaven have already thought to be mindful within their meditation of realisations amongst the constellations of the stars, that for their dreaming to unfold and become manifest, then such as it is, that wherever the Heavens begin to take root upon the birth places of Eden, then it is with this the Earth of the Adama that shall come forth to produce and re-establish a world anew.

AUTHORS NOTES

~*~

The Angel Babies Story for me, was very much written and inspired by many feelings of expression, that was buried very deeply inside of me, as it was through my own exchanges, and relationships, and journeying, and upon the discovery of both negative and positive experiences, that often challenged my own beliefs, and personal expectations of what I thought or felt was my own life's purpose, and reason for being and doing, and very much what any one of us would expect to be the result, or the outcome of their own personal life choices based upon the status quo of our own design or choosing.

The story within itself, very much maintains its own conception of intercession from one person to another, as we can only contain the comprehension of the things that we most relate too, and that which most commonly resembles and reflect our own emotions and experiences, by tying in with something tangible that either connects, or resonate at will deeply within us, as many of us have the ability and intuit nature, to grasp things not merely as they are presented to us, but how things can also unfold and manifest in us, that are sometimes far beyond our everyday imaginings, and that are also equally hard to grasp and somewhat difficult to comprehend and let alone explain.

As we often learn to see such challenges and difficulties as these, especially in young minds, that react in responsive ways and are also equally gifted, or equally find it in themselves in life changing circumstances, to deal with prevailing situations, that most of us would take for granted, and would naturally see as the average norm, as we are all somewhat uniquely adjusted to deal with the same prevailing situation very differently, or even more so to uniquely perceive it in very different ways.

As for the question of how we all independently learn to communicate through these various means of creative, or artistic, or spiritual measures, is also simply a way of communicating to God as in prayer, as well as with one another, as all aspects are one of the same creation, as to whether such forms of expression can personify, or act as an intermediate medium, or channel to God, or indeed from one person to another, is again very much dependent upon the nature of its composition and expression, and the root from which it extends, and so for us to believe that our forbearers, or indeed our ancestors have the ability to intercede for us in such spiritual terms upon this our journey through life, is very much to say, that it is through their life's experiences, that we have become equipped, and given a wealth, and a portion of their life's history, with which for us to make our own individual efforts and choices, for us to be sure and certain of the way, in which we shall eventually come to be.

When we take a leap of faith, it is often into the unknown, and it is often associated with, or stems from the result of our constant fate being applied and presented to us in the context of a fear or phobia, insomuch so, that we must somehow, or at least come face to face with, or deal with, or come to terms with these matters arising, that are usually our own personal concerns, or worries, or anxieties toward a balanced or foreseeable reality, which is often beyond our immediate control, in that we are attempting to define and deal with this systematic physical, and spiritual progression, in the hope and the faith that we can resolve these personal matters, so as to allow us to put the mind and the heart at ease and to rest.

As it is often through our rationalizing, and our affirmation, and our professing or living with our beliefs, that what we often call, or come to terms with through our acceptance, is that through faith, belief and worship in God, that such personal matters, can easily be addressed, and dealt with, so as to overcome when facing such difficult and challenging obstacles, as even when in response to a negative impact that can have a harmful effect upon our physical bodies and being, we also often rely upon this same faith in the physical terms of our living and well being to guide us, and especially where we are often engaged in rationalizing with this phenomena, in the context of our faith, hope and belief, which often requires and demands us to look upon the world in a completely different way, so that we can reach far beyond the rational expectations of our own reality, and perceive to look forward into that of our metaphysical world.

As it is through this metaphysical world of all irrationality, and chaos and confusion, that a leap of faith is required to pass through and beyond the unknown context of our rational and conscious reality, and thus so as far as we can see, to understand our consciousness, as we believe it should be, in that we are contained in every aspect of our faith, hope and belief, as we are often presented with more than just a rational imagination, of what lies beyond our eventful fate or worries and concerns, and so within the mind of dreams, we are presented with a super imagination, where extraordinary things exist and take effect much beyond our physical comprehension, although very much aligned to the interconnectedness within our emotions, that brings with it a super reality, where we can accept the tangibility of these dreams upon realizing them, so as to be found and understood, as when we are found to be waking up in our day to day reality and activity, but also in choosing not to deny or extinguish these dreams as mere dreams, but to accept, and to see them, or refer to them as signs.

As of when we see such tell tale signs, or such premonitions forgoing, or foreboding us in our fate, it is very much that these signs often impact the most upon that of our conscious minds, as they are very much presented to us in an informative and abstract way, very much like a picture puzzle that we are busily attempting to piece together and work out, and very much in the way that we are attempting to put the heart and the mind at ease and to rest, so as to secure peace of mind in order to find and establish and maintain inner peace, as such signs as these, are often the ones that I am referring too, and can often and easily be presented to us in many ways, but to be sure and certain, if they are Godly or Divining messages upon intuition and translation, very much depends and largely relies upon us as individuals, as to what we are naturally engaged in and pursuing, in the same hope and light of the context, of this experience of such a Godly nature.

As such experiences are crucial and key, as to how we deal with any or all relationships, especially when we are developing a relationship within the Godly aspects of our lives, as more often than not, when we use such phrases and metaphors as, 'Going through a Door' or 'Crossing a Bridge, it is simply by saying such statements as these, or putting things in this way or context, that we decidedly know and acknowledge that a big change is about to occur, and develop or happen to us, and so we in ourselves are becoming equipped and prepared to deal with such changes, as they shall determine what shall be the eventual outcome of our fate, as there may already have been so many foretelling signs, much before the final impact or infinite sign is presented to us, insomuch so, that it may have already been subtly presented to us, much before the true perspective or picture of our reality has come to fruition and presented to us as a whole.

The whole being, is that which pieces itself together, with all the necessary facets and aspects of our Human Nature, Personality, Mannerisms and Characteristics and Traits, as all in all, it presents to us a vision, which sets us apart from one another, but also equally ties us all together in the event and act of completing our picture and journey through life, and it is through these instincts that we all naturally possess, and is all that is inextricably woven into the metaphysical fabric and the spiritual aspects of the heart and mind, and of those that are channeled along the lines of the minds meridians, and the intricate channels that give way to apprehensible intuitive mental awareness of signs and dreams, and or premonitions or visions, of how, or what we may choose to accept, or to objectively analyze, or to take note of and perceive in communication, or indeed how God may choose to communicate with or through us.

As it is in our realizing that within our personal fate and decisiveness, that we are calling upon, and facing a reality, that questions and presents itself to us all, as something that is profoundly spiritual and ambiguous, in relation to what we are all intrinsically held and bound by within our faith and beliefs, in that what we expect is about to unravel itself before us, as we begin to discover all that in which we are, as such is the expectation and the realization in our phobias and fears, that we may begin to readdress or even regress, or desist in such a course of action concerning these doubts and deliberations, so as not to offset or to promote any ideas that may bring about any personal demise, or disharmony, or disunity, that may trigger any negative aspectual forecasts or emotions within ourselves, as it is such a self fulfilling reality, that we are all in subjection too, in creating along and upon our own individual paths of merits and natural progression, that naturally such phenomena is presented and revealed to us as a whole, and is often profoundly real and yet maintains its simplicity, and is quite ordinarily so upon our realization of it, as if by mere chance that somehow deep down we already knew, that when we became aware of it, we somehow knew it to be so.

As it is these lessons in life, that are to be learnt from such self affirming challenges, so as to test our minds imagination and of course that which is at the very heart, of how we in our Human nature, can so easily push our abilities far beyond the boundaries, upon the premise of what is, or what is not possible, which brings to mind the verse and saying of the scripture and that is to say, that if anyone adds or takes away from this book, then so too shall their part be added or taken away, and yet if we continue further along this point, it also goes on to ask, who is worthy to remove this seal, so as to reveal the dream or the foreknowledge that we may all come to terms with our natural agreement and acceptance of it, as it is in knowing and accepting what shall befall us in our fate, as to what choice of action we must or can take, as such are the phobias and fears of trepidation that also gives way to the rise of hope, so that we may come face to face with destiny.

As with each new day comes a new beginning, and with each new beginning comes new hopes and new expectations, as there are also new obstacles and challenges to overcome, as such is the dawning of life, to present to us all, such necessary and redeemable qualities within the observations of our lives, for to have hope, is to look up toward the heavens, and to quietly and silently know, that within this observation, that the sky or indeed the heavens, are still upheld by the forces of nature, that govern from above albeit much to our amazement and expectations, and that life is ordinarily and justly so, as we in our appreciation cannot always see beyond that which is so perfectly bound and set in motion with us in this universe, as we simply learn to believe and accept that this is the way of our living and all things besides us, as we are within all that has become created and laid out before us.

And yet with this new day dawning, if not for us to simply wake up and to use our hopes, and our aspirations to ascend beyond the obvious point of creation, and to apply our spiritual nature and positive will of motivation toward it, and it toward us upon reflection, as in our overcoming and prevailing, within its and our own destiny and deliverance, as such is also our descent to take warmth and courage, and comfort and refuge, when we lay down to take rest and sleep beneath the Moon and the Stars above, is also to take strength and peace of mind, in the hope and the understanding that a new day beginning, and a new dawning shall be presented to us once again, as this is the way of the life that we have come to know it, within our own divine ability and acceptance of it.

As much as life is and can very much be a challenge, it also appears to state, that there is a thread of universal commonality running through the whole of creation no matter what we profess to live and abide by as human beings, as for me the basis of these requirements that extend from this commonality is food, shelter, clothing, companionship, and a sense of connection or clarity derived from self awareness, that is not to say that there is not much more for broad scope beyond this basic measure and requirement that puts us all on an equal footing with one another, no matter where we inhabit or dwell in the world.

And so what and where are we permitted upon this universal basis, to gravitate towards, or indeed to excel to, in order to fulfill our existential experiences and engage with our full potential, as many of us in our progression towards modernity, would indeed interpretate this kind of idea or philosophy, depending upon which part of the world we lived in or inhabited, as being very much viewed differently realized upon that same broad basis, which also brings me to ask, and to question, and to examine this brave new world within this context, or indeed as some would profess to say or mention, within this new world order, or new world system, as there is much to address and to consider for all concerned.

For once we have evolved and grown and matured away from our basic needs and requirements, it would also appear that many of us who have indeed excelled, or concluded in the context of a post-modernistic era of environment or society, to have almost achieved something, which is of a value, or at least on a par with something that is equally attributed, to that of a spiritual level of attainment, or indeed enlightenment, but when we address the cost of such achievement, we also begin to see that we are still somewhat grounded in our best efforts by this basic requirement, which is to achieve, acquire, and survive at will, and to endure, and to live, and to abide by such new discoveries of achievements.

As even in this progress and achievement of what we would wish, or presume to call a new world, how do we fairly address or balance, or differentiate between those of us who are yet to grasp the basis of this understanding that is required for us to excel, or indeed for us to fly, or indeed to reach the highest spiritual level of attainment of understanding, of being, doing, and knowing, as in realizing that indeed not many of us could have, or would have had the opportunity, or indeed the privilege, of exercising such expressions of freedom in our new found world.

As some of us are fundamentally held by the very conventions of what is required upon this, a basic level of our independence, maintenance, and survival, to regulate and maintain the simplicity of ourselves, and yet once we have experienced and entertained this new idea inside such a concept, our first response is how should we, or what should we do in order to engage with one another, to bring about its universality as a basic principle and as a must for all concerned, and how can it be any good for us, if indeed we all profoundly have separate agendas, or different ideals, as to what should, or could take precedence over the basic and fundamental needs to live out our lives, when food, and shelter, and clothing, and companionship, and a sense of self, or a clarity of awareness is needed at the very heart of what it is, to not only be, but remain humane.

As for the background, or indeed the backdrop, and the combining and dedicated efforts, that it has taken me as a writer to come to arrive at within this story of the Angel Babies, and of course the time that it has taken for me, to construct, and to collate the necessary, and if I may say worthy and worthwhile aspects, for this particular body of work to become written and completed within the trilogy of the Angel Babies, I would very much like just like to inform the readership, that upon exploration and construction of this body of work, that I myself as a person, have experienced several variables of conversions upon my spiritual and emotional being, upon the instruction and initiation of bringing the series of these books into the light.

For had I not been introduced into the many schools of thought and allied faiths of Christianity, Islam, Hare Krsna, Hindu, Buddhism, Dao and Shinto, that it may never have transpired or surmounted, or indeed would have been very much an arduous and challenging task, to find the right motivation for the narrative, very much needed and applied, with which to find and devise the relative inspiration, and ideas explored and written within the context and narrative of the characters and the storyline that I have presented to you as an author.

~ Clive Alando Taylor

REFERENCE

~*~

Edward Tyler - (1832 – 1917)
A Soul - Anima
R. R. Marett - (1866 – 1943)
A Soul - **Animism/Animatism**
A Soul - **Otahchuk**/North American **Algonquian Indians**
Tetra Valley-(Fictional Place)
The Doctrine of - **(Samsara)**
i.e **A former life influences the present one**
Jiva- (**Hindu** term for the personal Soul or being)
Cavea - (Cage)
Kali Ma - (**Hindu Supreme Goddess** or **Black Earth Mother**)
Empyrean - (Heaven/Angelic Dwelling Place)
Celestial Abode - (Infinite Heaven/ Angelic Dwelling Place)
Haven - (Inner Sanctuary, Peace)
Mercidiah - (Fictional Earth Mother)
Josephine - (Younger Fictional Earth Mother)
Men Shen - (Taoist Interpretation meaning/Guardians of the Door)
Qonshushmigns - Conscious Minds/Truth/ Reality
Hark the Herald - (The Listening Angel)
Angel Zyxven - (Agreement/Covenant/Spirit)
Angel Satan / Leviathan - (Bright & Morning Star)
Ophlyn the Herald Angel - (The Fallen Angel)
Angel Ruen - (The Avenging Angel)
Angel of Justice - (figuratively)
Angel of Mercy - (figuratively)

Angel Pablo - (The Eternal Angel)
Angel Stefan - (Love)
Nejeru - (New Jerusalem)
Several Worlds - (Future Event)

BIBLIOGRAPHY

~*~

Mankind's Search For God
Watch Tower Bible
And **Tract Society of Pennsylvania** 1990
Brooklyn New York. INC
International Bible Studies Association
~ Time Has Every Ending No Destiny ~
T . H . E . E . N . D
Angelus Domini
A **Tao.House** Product/**AngelBabies IIII**
LEVIATHAN / 2014
For further info contact Clive: **tao.house@live.co.uk**
A Fountain Of Love Valentine Production
tao.house@live.co.uk
Copyright: 2014 Clive Alando Taylor

~*~